Gohar Kordi lives in London with her husband and her 11-year-old son. Her story, 'From Missionary School to Mitcham', appeared in the anthology *So Very English* (1990); and her autobiographical novel, *An Iranian Odyssey*, was published the following year (1991). She has written a television film script called *An Iranian Childhood* (1993). Her story, 'I Was Touched', appeared in *Mustn't Grumble: Writing by Disabled Women* (The Women's Press, 1994); and she has also written a short story, 'Hold the Word', for *Brought to Book* (1994). She is currently working on a stage play and another novel.

$\mathcal{M}ahi's$

STORY

Gohar Kordi

First published by The Women's Press Ltd, 1995
A member of the Namara Group
34 Great Sutton Street, London EC1V 0DX

British Library Cataloguing-in-Publication Data
A catalogue record for this book is available from the British
Library

ISBN 0 7043 4373 8

Typeset in Palatino by Contour Typesetters, Southall, London
Printed and bound in Great Britain by
BPC Paperbacks Ltd, Aylesbury, Bucks

To the memory of my mother, Mahi

Acknowledgements

I would like to warmly thank the following people for their involvement in completing this book: Helen Windrath, at The Women's Press, for her invaluable editorial help; Jean, for having patiently typed the manuscript; and my husband David, for his moral support. Thank you all for your encouragement.

Contents

Contents

Author's Foreword

> If you find something good share it with anyone you can find. In that way the goodness will spread, no telling how far it will go.
>
> Forest Carter
> *The Education of the Little Tree*

In this book I would like to share with you the good things I remember from my childhood, the good things I have discovered about my mother, and the good things about the little village in Iran where I was born.

My first book, *An Iranian Odyssey*, is autobiographical and deals with the events of the first twenty years of my life. When it was published in 1991, I had no idea what to expect, what people would think. The reception it received was far beyond my wildest dreams. It was widely reviewed and highly praised here in England, in Germany, and later in the United States. *An Iranian Odyssey* was also shortlisted for the Elizabeth Frink Award and the Fawcett Society Book Prize, and adapted for radio and television.

In that book I focused on my early life, and I expressed particular anger towards my mother and her treatment of me. The reviewers reacted strongly, calling her a brutal and cruel mother. Friends and acquaintances judged her harshly and talked critically of her. This did not feel right to me. Deep down I began to realise that I had not done her justice, because of my intense anger with her and the way I had expressed it. The image that had come over of her as a villain, a monster, someone entirely evil, seemed to me to be ultimately unjust, unreal, distorted. I felt responsible for this and I knew that I had to do something to put it right. I decided to write this book, focusing this time on my mother's life events and experiences. In this way I hoped to clear up the misunderstandings and misconceptions about her. Now that I had let out my anger and written about the many negative feelings that I had stored away for all those years, I knew that I could stand back and give a more positive, balanced picture of her and, by so doing, give a balanced picture of my own past. Now I could see her in a different light. I began to understand how my mother had fought vigorously throughout her short life for some degree of independence within the patriarchal system. As a child I witnessed her being beaten up by her husband, by her younger brother and later by her son. She had been terrorised and exploited by the landlord. She had been married at the age of twelve against her will and then divorced by her husband for not allowing the marriage to be consummated. She was a brave, strong and determined woman, a fighter. She died at the age of 45 from exhaustion, burnt out by the hardships of her life. I am proud of her and feel privileged to have re-discovered her in the writing of this book. And I hope I have redressed the balance.

Many readers and reviewers of my first book also felt that it had been critical of Iranian society. I recall how once during an interview about *An Iranian Odyssey* I was asked, 'How did you manage to carry on, what gave you strength?' I felt at the time that I did not answer this question adequately but it got me thinking that there must have been something positive in my life, enabling me to carry on, to survive. What was it? Bit by bit things came back to me, good things about my past, my childhood, about my mother. I remembered mother's pride in me as a little girl, how I was loved, cherished and admired by her. And I recalled the care and appreciation I had received in my village from the whole community. 'Whose daughter is this? But she is beautiful,' comments from passers-by which filled mother with pride. I remembered the joys of life in my village in the countryside – how I had played freely in the river, in the hills and in the fields with the animals, recalling the pleasure and excitement I had felt. Even after losing my sight, no restrictions were placed on me. I was given total freedom and trusted like any other child. I felt at one with nature, exposed to all the elements. I feel that being valued as a child, unconditionally and by the whole community, was the source of my strength, of my survival. It enabled me to retain my faith in human nature. And I strongly feel that the reason mother managed to endure so much in life and survive as long as she did was because she herself had been valued as a child, as indeed all children are in that society.

Such memories made me decide that I wanted to write about these very positive aspects of Iranian life and culture. I wanted to give a picture of village life as I had experienced it, depicting the community's value system, way of life, and treatment of children. In particular, I felt that I should acknowledge the way I was treated and cared for in that community, and the beneficial effects this had for me. Without this, no fair assessment of my past could emerge. I felt indebted and this needed to be expressed. I feel I have given a fuller, more complete picture now than I did in my first book.

Writing this book I rediscovered many aspects of my early life in Iran, but most importantly I got to know my mother. This book is a tribute to her and to all women of her calibre.

Gohar Kordi

4

New Life

The evening was drawing in. Mahi felt happy, exuberant, she glowed with pleasure. In fact, she felt on top of the world. She did not understand why this was so, she just felt happy. She had just returned from a very long stay with her parents in Khorbendeh, a fairly distant village, a day's journey on a donkey. Now the visit seemed far behind her. Now she couldn't remember why she had gone away for such a time. She felt strange that she had been away for so long from her home, her husband, her friends, her own environment. She felt very much at ease here. This was her home. Her family. She felt a little girlish. Slightly embarrassed at having stayed with her mum for nearly two months. Now she felt such a totally different person. She felt full of life and energy, her face glowed with pleasure, her eyes sparkled, she was always smiling, she laughed heartily and often. The whole time she bubbled, vibrated, she was active day and night, she was swift and light in her movements. She felt she could lift up the whole earth in her arms and replace it with the moon if she wanted to. She felt she could catch the stars one by one, play with them, throw them about, catch them again, just as she played with pebbles by the river. She loved to watch the stars in the night, especially the summer nights when the family slept on the roof for the coolness. She would lie awake for hours watching the stars, counting them, playing with them, catching them, holding them, carrying them and being carried on them great distances to unknown lands. She dreamt often of being carried away with them. Now she felt the whole planet was in her control and she could do with it whatever she desired.

'Mahi, are you home?' It was Khoshghadam her neighbour, calling over the wall.

'Yes, I am. What is it, Khoshghadam?'

'Just a moment.' And Khoshghadam was over within a minute. 'I have cooked *kachee*, I have brought you a taste.'

'Oh, you shouldn't have bothered, Khoshghadam,' said Mahi with a giggle. But she thanked her and took the covered bowl from her.

'It's aromatic, you see, I thought you might like some.'

Mahi dropped her head shyly, avoiding her friend's gaze.

'Mahi, look at me,' Khoshghadam said. She looked into her eyes and saw the secret Mahi had been trying to hide. 'Tell me what is going on?'

'What is going on? I don't know what you are talking about, Khoshghadam,' Mahi twinkled. She made as if to wipe the sweat from her forehead, hiding behind her scarf as she did so.

'You have changed so much since you came back from Khorbendeh.'

'Nothing is going on,' Mahi giggled, shifting her steps. 'I was just going to call you actually, it's time to go and fetch water, isn't it?'

'You are trying to change the subject,' Khoshghadam said smiling. 'We'll go and fetch water in a minute. First, you tell me what is going on?'

'I don't know what you're talking about,' Mahi said quickly, giggling again.

'You see, since you've been back over the last three days, you haven't stopped for a minute, constantly going from one thing to another. You've done your own spring-cleaning, helped with mine and that of Tahereh and Zahra, it's as though you want to renew the whole world. And you are full of energy, full of enthusiasm. So lively and full of vitality. I have never seen you like this before!'

Mahi blushed. 'Yes, this is how I feel. I like doing things.'

'There must be a reason for it, what is it?' She looked her in the eye again for a moment, as the two women connected with each other, in each other, right inside in a world where all the secrets are kept, even from themselves at times.

'Mahi, you are pregnant.'

Mahi's face lit up, her eyes twinkled. She opened her arms and the two women embraced. Together they sighed with relief. Now it had surfaced, had been acknowledged, put into words.

Mahi was not yet eighteen and she had a three-year-old son, Ali, her first child. She was proud, having given birth to a boy first. Male children were so highly valued. A daughter would marry and go to the husband's family but Ali, he would stay with his parents, and would look after them in their old age.

Mahi had been married before, at the age of twelve, against her will. The marriage had not been consummated. 'Over my dead body,' she was reported as saying. She had been divorced by him as was his right as a husband refused services.

So, this was her second marriage. Again against her will, she had been married to Reza. He was ten years older than herself, a Turk from a faraway village. By the failure of the first marriage she had brought shame upon the family, but this didn't stop her resisting the second one for some time! Reza had been patient with her. 'She'll come round,' he had said to his sister, Zolikha, who had been monitoring the consummation on the wedding night, together with Mahi's mother. He had been gentle with her.

She had always been a rebellious girl. She was the third

7

child of five – three boys and two girls. The oldest, a boy, Habib, was a bully and cruel to his sisters and brothers. Mahi had persistently defied him and so had always been in trouble with him. The second child, Khadijeh, a girl, had married and been raped by her husband on the wedding night. From then on she had refused to sleep with him ever again. She had become pregnant, been divorced, had given birth to a girl, and had later had a breakdown from which she had never recovered. Mahi was the third child. The fourth was a boy, Ezatollah, and the fifth, the last, also a boy, Hassan.

Having been used to standing up to Habib, her oldest brother, Mahi did not have difficulty in showing her dislike for Reza. He was too weak in her view, and moreover he had married a divorcee. Why had he come all this way and chosen her? He wasn't even from her own people, a Kurd. He was a Turk, foreign as far as she was concerned. Totally unsuitable, and much older than her, ten years older. She had not known his parents, they had died and she was not interested in how or when. He had a brother, Noroozgholi, who lived with his family in a Turkish village, half a day's donkey ride away. Reza also had two sisters, Zolikha and Asli, who lived with their families in the same village as Mahi. She was on good terms with his sisters, friends with them, but at the same time she kept her distance, not giving them a chance to interfere in her life. She would choose her own friends and confide in whoever she wanted. The brother, Noroozgholi, was a quiet, gentle, generous man. Whenever he visited he brought presents for the family, especially the children. She liked him, and Zolikha the older sister who was kind, caring and non-interfering. Zolikha was well-respected in the community and many addressed her as 'Aunt Zolikha'. Young women would seek her advice and help, she was one of the village's wise women. But Asli, the youngest, a very lively energetic young woman with whom Mahi had a good laugh could be interfering. With her she felt she had to protect herself at times. They helped each other a lot, especially when they had to weave a carpet, or do the spring-cleaning. But Mahi was cautious of getting too close.

She liked the sisters and the brother of her husband, the only person she was not fond of was the husband himself! And especially lately when Mahi had become somewhat bored and at times frustrated, as though she was not being stretched enough now that her boy Ali was older and she did not have to do so much for him. She found herself getting into arguments with her husband and refusing to do things for him such as repairing his trousers. 'It is as though I haven't got a wife,' Reza would jokingly comment to his friends, pointing to the hole in his trouser knees. But Mahi took no notice. 'I don't care,' she would murmur to herself and turn away as though she had not heard the conversation. She would not take orders. She would do things of her own free will and in her own time.

But now, everything had changed. She couldn't understand why she had not been kind to Reza, not even patching up his trousers, this was the least she could do for him, she was his wife after all. And all those arguments where she shouted and he kept quiet! Now life was totally different for her. She rejoiced at the thought of being pregnant again, and she could not in all honesty find anything to dislike in Reza. He had always been gentle with her, respectful and loving.

Mahi was small, dainty, petite, not a particularly beautiful woman but she had charisma, and it was her character that attracted people. She was strong, decisive, determined, very capable and adventurous, willing to try anything. She was artistic, and made beautiful carpets. Her choice of colour and design was exquisite, very special, everyone said so. She had her own style. She only had to put her mind to something to make it a big success. All the carpets she made belonged to the landlord, but she enjoyed making them, and took pleasure in mixing and playing around with the colours and experimenting with the

9

designs. This would give her enormous joy. She was especially good at sewing. Many of her friends brought their *chadors* for her to cut for them. Cutting *chadors* was a very difficult task, not everyone could do it and no one in the village could do it as well as she did. She was also an excellent cook. Khoshghadam would often remark, 'Mahi, I don't know how you do it. You make the most wonderful meals from next-to-nothing!'

Early one morning Mahi and Khoshghadam, her sisters-in-law, Asli and Zolikha, and a few other friends, all with their children, took to the hillsides for herb gathering. They would have to start early so as to return to the village before mid-day when the sun would be at its highest, otherwise the heat would be too much for them. They made this journey a few times each season, in the spring, summer and autumn, except winter when the hills would be covered with snow. Each time they went they would look for different kinds of herbs, at different stages of growth. Zolikha was usually one of the group, as she was somewhat older than the others and they looked to her experience and expertise. She would tell them all about the kinds of herbs and their properties, and they would learn how to treat, dry, store, and use them. Some of the herbs had to have the oil extracted from them, and the young women would be shown how to do this by the older women.

That day Mahi collected many different bunches of herbs. The women laughed and joked, they ran and played and had just as much fun as their children who played alongside. Mahi and Khoshghadam chased each other over the hills. At times the women would separate from the group and go off in twos or threes, or at times go on their own for a while, and call to each other over the hills, listening to their echoes. They took food, sweets and drinks with them. They had fun, they shared everything, their work, their problems, their complaints, their joy, in everything they were together and this was their strength.

The women from their village always worked in small groups, they did almost everything in each other's company, whether it was sewing, spinning or weaving, they would work away for hours in their friends' houses. Or they would go, together, with their washing to the riverside or to the spring and spend a whole day there, washing and drying on the stones. Some women had their babies strapped on their backs as they worked. They would have fun, make a day of it. Their laughter and chatter mixing with the running of water over the stones. They did little work on their own. When they had major cleaning to do in the house, such as spring-cleaning or whitewashing, they went to each other for help. They worked in twos and threes, and in this way not only was the work finished much quicker, but they had fun in doing it. This was the important part, having fun. In spring-cleaning they would get out all the contents of the house, then they would clean everything, wash, air, repair, whitewash the house and put everything back all refreshed, repaired, and renewed. They would do this before and after each winter as well as in summer. Towards the end of autumn the men would attend to the roofs, an extra layer of clay would be applied onto the roof to give extra protection so that they would be well prepared for the heavy winter snows.

Although Mahi was enjoying herself that day on the hills gathering herbs, somehow she felt she wanted to get back as soon as possible. She could not understand why this was but it was as though something was waiting for her, she felt she had to go home. She was a bit restless.

'We must be going back soon, girls,' she called out to Khoshghadam and Zahra, who were playing with the children on top of the hill, running up and down with them.

'What's the matter with you today, Mahi?' Khoshghadam called.

'What do you want to get home for? Let us enjoy ourselves in this beautiful countryside with all these beautiful wild flowers around us, what do you want to go home for? Come on, join in, what are you doing there sitting all by yourself?'

Mahi did not answer, she sat down, her herbs next to her wrapped in a cloth. She went back to her thoughts, daydreaming, as she often did lately, her daydreams so sweet and appealing, so satisfying. 'I have a little girl inside me, a little girl. I'm going to have a little girl this time, a beautiful little girl. I'll make the most beautiful clothes for her to wear, my little angel. She will be born near *Norooz* . . . wouldn't it be interesting if she was born on *Norooz* Day, the New Year, itself?' She giggled to herself at the thought of it. 'I don't know anyone who has had a baby on *Norooz* Day. It would be wonderful to be the first to give birth on the day itself. Oh God, please make it happen. I'll make a vow, if I give birth on *Norooz* Day. I will make halva every Friday evening and give it to all the neighbourhood.' So this time it would be a girl. A little girl! An image of herself. She would do anything for her. She would make it possible for her to have all the things that she herself had not had. She would not force her to marry anyone that she did not want to, no, she wouldn't do what her mother had done to her. 'She will be free like the birds, just like these birds,' she said to herself. 'Look how free, how light they are. No one has put any burden on them. No restrictions, no conditions, they can go anywhere they want and mix with anyone they want, with nothing to stop them. Look at them.' She watched the birds overhead, following their flights as far as she could. High on the hill as she was she could look over the whole village in the valley. How beautiful it looked. 'My little daughter will be like that little bird on the branch of that tree on the farside of the village. I can just see it, it is beautiful and free. Such is the freedom I want my daughter to have, I will make sure of it.'

'Where are you, Mahi, are you dreaming again? We're off.' laughed Khoshghadam, patting her on the back. 'If we had all gone and left you here all alone, you wouldn't have noticed, would you? You are in another world,' she said, squeezing her on both shoulders.

When Mahi got home she unpacked her herbs, had a wash, got some lunch ready. Khoshghadam and her little boy were having lunch with her and her son, Ali. She quickly fetched a bowl of yoghurt, put it into a larger bowl, diluted it with water, mixing the water gently in as she stirred then beat it fast until it changed into a thinnish soup consistency. Then she added a pinch of salt, some washed, chopped herbs from the garden – mint, chives, radishes, rosemary, spring onions, and parsley, together with a few tiny cucumbers, and raisins and walnuts. Mahi mixed it all and now it was quite thick. Then she opened the *sofreh*, the cloth in which she kept the bread wrapped, and broke some bread. She chose the thin, crispy bits, broke them so that they were like crumbs and added them to the bowl. All four of them washed their hands, spread the *sofreh* and then sat on the floor around it, putting the bowl in the middle with one spoon in it. All four of them ate from the same bowl, sharing the one spoon. They talked and laughed as they ate.

Suddenly Mahi heard a crow cawing away on the wall. It cawed three times. 'You may bring the good news, crow. What good news have you got for me this time?' Mahi exclaimed with excitement. And a little later the crow again cawed three times. And again and again. Mahi was sure that it was a good sign, crows did not caw for nothing. Whenever they came they carried good news, and it was sitting on her wall after all, so she must expect that something good would happen.

Khoshghadam agreed with her. 'It normally means that someone will arrive from far away.'

'I wonder who is coming?' Mahi said.

'Well, your brothers or your mother, maybe?'

'Oh no, I don't think so,' Mahi said. 'It is not yet a week since I returned from Khorbendeh. I sent news to mother that I am alright. She won't visit me for a few more weeks.'

13

'Well someone is coming from somewhere.'

'Perhaps Reza's brother, Noroozgholi, will drop in,' Mahi said in anticipation.

They thoroughly enjoyed the lunch and then Mahi made some tea and they sat chatting away non-stop and sorting out their herbs, cleaning, washing and cutting them, ready for drying the next day. Early in the morning they would spread a clean cloth on the roof and put the herbs on it, each in a different patch. By early evening they would be bone-dry, and then Mahi and Khoshghadam would put them all into separate well-sealed containers and store them.

That whole day Mahi was excited. She was sure that someone was arriving from far away to visit her. The crow had not failed her yet. So that evening she decided she would cook rice with noodles. She had cut the noodles herself the day before and they were hanging in the room to dry, some very fine and some thick ones. The thick spaghetti-type ones she would use in the soup. But the thin ones, fine as egg noodles, she would use in rice. She made a fire in the fireplace in the yard, filled her heavy copper pot with water, placed it over the heat and, when it came to the boil, put in the well-washed rice. After a quick boil she added the noodles and some salt, and when she thought it was right, she strained it through a cane rice strainer. Mahi then put some oil into the pot, and while this heated, she peeled a good-sized potato, slicing it into large thin slices, before putting them at the bottom of the pan and covering it. Then she put the rice back in the pot, with a couple of spoonfuls of water sprinkled on top, covered the pot again with a round thick cushion, which she used to keep in the steam and at the same time absorb the excess moisture. To tell when it was ready she wet her finger and touched the back of the pot. It made a hissing noise which meant the rice was ready. Then she put some cold water on the ground and put the pot on the wet patch. This helped the crust at the bottom to come loose easily. Then before serving she heated some more oil and sprinkled it on top.

She kept looking out whilst she did all this. She always left her front door open, as did everybody else, but this time she was expecting someone. Then it all happened. There it was. A donkey was being led in. It was her mother on the donkey. Roghiieh had come to visit her. She rushed towards her with open arms, shouting, 'Mother, you! I really didn't expect to see you so soon – how wonderful! The crow has been cawing all day.' And the two women embraced. Mahi hid her head in her mother's bosom. The two women were silent for a few moments, just hugging each other with only a 'Dear mother', 'Dear Mahi', murmured between them.

Now Ali had arrived from next door where he had been playing with his friend, having heard his mother's scream of jubilation and was pulling at Grandma's *chador*. The women let go of each other. Roghiieh picked up Ali in her arms and kissed him heartily on both cheeks a few times, whispering endearments to him. After a good hug she put him down and out of her pocket brought a handful of goodies for him to eat, raisins mixed with walnuts, almonds and sweets. Ali rushed next door to share it with his friend.

Mahi stood facing her mother as though she was not quite sure whether this was a dream or if it was really happening. She rubbed her eyes to make sure. This really was her mother, she wasn't dreaming. She dreamt a lot, everyone said so. But this was real, she was there in the flesh in front of her. How lucky she was, what a wonderful surprise, this was the best treat she could ever have expected.

Roghiieh looked her in the eyes, a moment of inspection, penetrating right to her inner self. In a flash she understood, her daughter was pregnant! 'Mahi, you're pregnant,' she said out loud, and they embraced again, sighing at each other and hugging each other tight, feeling each other's heart beat. Roghiieh was proud, her daughter was pregnant again. Fertility in animals, land, or people, was highly praised and prized, especially by mothers in the case of their own daughters, this was very special.

That night mother and daughter lay together on the roof and whispered for a long time. Reza left the roof to the two women and slept down in the yard. It was well after midnight before they fell asleep. There had been a lot to talk about. Roghiieh had told Mahi that she had had a dream about her, and that was why she had come to make sure everything was all right. 'Now I see what my dream was about,' she told her with a joy in her voice.

Roghiieh wanted to go back to her village the next day. Mahi persuaded her with great difficulty to stay two more days. Mother and daughter were inseparable. Roghiieh had cried on the occasion of both of her daughters' wedding nights, as did most mothers. Mahi had tried to hide her tears, and Roghiieh had tried to leave the room or turn her face away when the tears came. They had a very special relationship, mother and daughter, they felt each other's pain from afar, and they often dreamt about each other, especially at the time of important events.

It was the evening of the day Roghiieh left that Mahi saw the full moon. 'Blessings,' she uttered at the sight of it. Then she looked in the pond water as was the custom, the first thing she should see after the full moon should be water or her reflection in the mirror, if she saw a human face it should be a nice face, a positive one. If it happened to be a bad face, an unhappy sour face, then she would have bad luck until the end of that month. She climbed the ladder and with a thick nail made a hole in the wall under the gutter. From now on at the sight of each full moon, she would make one more hole in the wall until the birth of her child. She could remember the number of months anyway but she had heard that some of the young women had done it and so she wanted to do it too, it was a kind of fashion, something new, interesting. When she had told her mother about it she had laughed, 'My dear Mahi,' she had said, 'I always remembered my months of pregnancy and knew exactly when I was going to give birth, for five pregnancies, without making holes in the walls.'

'Yes, but what if one does forget,' Mahi had replied, laughingly. But underneath she knew she was doing this just for the fun of it.

Oh how she had always hated being married to Reza! She had hated the sight of him, had dreaded having sex with him. Those moments of intercourse when Reza would corner her somehow and force her to do it, had been such an ordeal. She hated it beyond recognition. In those moments she loathed all men, the whole process revolted her. Some occasions she found more of an ordeal than others. The last had been one of those. Now, come to think of it, the last intercourse had resulted in this, her pregnancy, such a wonderful thing which filled her with such a joy. 'What a world,' she said to herself, smiling, 'One thing of horror results in another of joy and in such a short time too, one moment you are living a nightmare and the next you are in jubilation and they are both connected, one act resulting in the other. I don't understand these things!'

The arguments between her and her husband seemed so petty now. She had been just a foolish girl. Nothing justified getting so worked up and being so rude to poor Reza, she admitted to herself. 'I shall make something nice for dinner tonight to please him, I'll show him what I can do for him, he loves his food.' So that evening she cooked him his favourite dish, rice cooked with lentils, sprinkled with raisins and in the middle with dates, and chunks of meat on top. The aroma could be smelt many houses away.

'Poor Reza,' she thought, after they had eaten. 'He is not a bad man really. I feel a bit sorry for him. How he keeps quiet when I refuse to do anything for him. What kind of a woman am I? And his wanting to have sex with me, it is after all his right.' Mother said many times, 'It is the kind of urge they feel and they must have it.' 'Just close your eyes, don't think about it,' she had said to her on her wedding night. 'Let him get on with it, it will be over in a few moments.' And now that seemed such a small price to pay for this pregnancy.

Physical sexual pleasure for her with Reza did not exist. On the contrary, it was all pain, disgust, horror. But in her dreams she experienced the most beautiful sexual pleasure which would roll over her, drowning her, sinking deep inside her, lifting her right above, as she floated free, especially when she imagined she was with one particular childhood sweetheart. It felt deliciously satisfying, nourishing, enriching. She often indulged herself in these dreams and fantasies, be it in her sleep at night, or while her thoughts wandered in the day.

In real life Mahi flirted from time to time with men who appealed to her. One young man who she fancied was Mohamad, a distant cousin of her husband. Mohamad visited them often, he was attracted to Mahi too, and both secretly experienced the other's desire. Sometimes when Mahi thought of him she longed to be in his arms. One day Mohamad had visited unexpectedly, Khoshghadam had witnessed their meeting. Reza was not around that day. Mohamad had knocked on the door. 'Is anybody home?' he called out. 'Reza, Mahi, Ali?' But nobody answered. Mahi was at Khoshghadam's giving her a hand in churning the butter. Mohamad knocked harder on the door and called out louder. Mahi, who had been chattering and laughing loudly and heartily, had not heard him the first time though Mohamad had recognised her voice, her laughter, from the village square. He knew she must be next door. He'd walked towards Khoshghadam's house, through the gate. He could hear the women's voices, Mahi's full of joy and enthusiasm for life. He called out, 'Is anybody at home?' This time Mahi heard him, she recognised his voice instantly and rushed out towards him. She ran full speed and open armed to embrace him, kissing him on both cheeks passionately.

'Mahi, you hugged and kissed Mohamad with such a passion, it reminded me of all those love stories we know. I didn't believe that it could happen in reality. I thought that kind of meeting only existed in stories,' Khoshghadam would tease.

'You love to go on about this, Khoshghadam, don't you?' Mahi laughed in reply.

Khoshghadam did not stop teasing her about this, and they would joke about it, but they kept it to themselves.

Although Mahi really disliked any sexual encounter with her husband, she could talk about it with such an appetite when it concerned other young women.

'What were you up to last night Khoshghadam, hey? You didn't come on to the roof last night, you and Hussein, for some time. You were up to something, weren't you, ah ha ha?' she would chuckle.

'I don't know what you are talking about, Mahi. I wasn't up to anything, you must be thinking of your own doings. I don't know what Reza has been doing to you, you can't stop thinking about "doings" and "goings on".'

Mahi loved teasing other young women about their sex life and took great pleasure in joking with them about it. She often sang love songs, she flirted with other young men, she dreamt a lot, she told love stories to her friends and listened to theirs with great enthusiasm. Her sensuality attracted her to, and had an immediate effect on, other men.

But of course she was very loyal to her family. As a woman with a child she could not have conceived of leaving her family. She looked after her little boy, very proud of her male firstborn. With great care she would make him beautiful clothes, play with him a great deal, change him often, wanting to keep him clean and spotless. She remembered how proud she had been to be pregnant, the reverence with which she as a mother-to-be had been regarded. It was the highest form of creativity. What higher state could a woman achieve than that of pregnancy, childbirth, motherhood? She remembered how she and her friends as little girls, as early as two or three, practised for motherhood; with dolls to begin with, and then with younger babies. She would dress herself up as if she were grown up, putting on her mother's *chador*, folding it many times, and wearing her shoes. She would pretend to be a real mother, mimicking exactly the way her own mother behaved towards her. Mahi remembered how she would dress her dolls and talk to them:

'Now it is time for you to feed; now it is time to go to sleep; now it is time to get up; now it is time to have a wash; here is some milk for you; I'm just going to milk the goats,' she would say. 'Now I'm going to bake the bread, you just sit here and I'll give you a nice piece of bread to eat, be careful not to burn your hand, it's hot.'

She would wash her doll, groom her, make her clothes. Dolls were the only toys made for the little girls. Mahi's had been made by her mother out of cloth, which she had stuffed, and for which she had made colourful clothes and costumes. Mahi would follow her mother around the house with the doll, copying everything that her mother did. She sang the doll to sleep just as her mother sang to her. She nursed the doll, nurtured it just as she had been nursed and nurtured, and motherhood became her highest ambition.

Mahi cast her mind back to previous pregnancies and childbirths which she had experienced. Like any other young girl, she had witnessed childbirth many times over, with her mother, relatives and neighbours. She knew that during the birth the house would fill up with people coming in and out, all women. Grandma or an aunt would come and stay with them for a long time to look after the mother and baby. It was a time of celebration, jubilation. Giving birth came to be associated with immense pleasure and happiness and was regarded as the greatest event in the women's lives.

Mahi thought blissfully about her own first pregnancy, how much attention she had received, all the fuss that had been made of her. The child she was carrying, she had been told, was a gift from God, and both the child and the carrier, the woman, were very special. She remembered how special she was made to feel, and how well looked after she had been by everyone. By nurturing her, it was believed, the baby would be nurtured through her. She remembered how the whole community had rejoiced with her, and how she had been thoroughly spoiled. The house had been full of people, a non-stop procession of visitors. Neighbours, friends and relatives all made delicacies, and brought her a little to try. For the wellbeing of the child, it was essential that she should be happy. She must have fun. Bad news was not talked about in front of her, anything which might bring about bad feelings or thoughts would be avoided, only positive and happy things were to be discussed in front of her. She should not be in the company of barren women, and everything she saw should be giving, yielding, productive, creative. Old disputes were forgotten and forgiven, any resentments put to one side, all to ease Mahi's pregnancy and birthing.

She recalled how in the summer of her early pregnancy she experienced *viar* or cravings for certain delicacies. Her craving had been for quinces. How hard it had been to find them, being winter fruit, but Reza had found one for her, after a great search.

'I have travelled many miles to find this for you,' he'd said in front of her friend Khoshghadam with laughter.

She remembered how she got the best of everything in those nine monts of her pregnancy and for some time after giving birth to allow her to recuperate. She enjoyed thoroughly this period of her life which was life-giving, loving, lavishing. Any resentments or disputes with her were forgiven and forgotten.

With *viar*, Mahi indulged in all kinds of desires and allowed herself to be spoilt. The pregnancy legitimised her greed and unlimited desire for food of any variety and any amount. She thrived on all this attention, appreciation and affirmation. She was showered with good things to eat, good feelings, good thoughts towards her, all with utmost generosity. She remembered too how whenever she went into a house her presence was valued because as a pregnant woman it was felt she would bring good luck with her.

For her first baby all the clothing and things were provided by her mother, all beautifully made from the finest cotton suitable for a newborn's delicate skin. Her mother came a few days before the birth and stayed with her for forty days as was the custom. She took over the running of the house, giving complete rest to Mahi and teaching her to look after the baby, especially as this was the first one. Roghiieh had brought her best oil with her, saved especially for the visit, to give to her daughter. She believed that oily food was particularly good for pregnant women. 'It will build you up, help you through the birth,' she had told Mahi. Mahi knew with her second pregnancy that her mother's stay would be shorter, only a week or so.

Mahi had enjoyed to the full this enormous extravagance and generosity, these loving, caring feelings all around her engulfing her and her baby son. This undoubtedly put enormous resources within her, providing a strength and richness from which she could later give to her first-born child, and from which she could carry on giving for years to come. This wealth laid the foundation for her and her baby.

Now Mahi was thrilled to be enjoying all this once more. Gradually the nine months was coming to an end, and *Norooz* was approaching. Before *Norooz* everyone spring-cleaned, whitewashed the houses, made new clothes. If adults could not afford new clothes for themselves, somehow they made sure that the children got them. It was imperative that they should have at least something new for *Norooz*. Everything should be refreshed and renewed.

Delicacies and sweets were made, eggs coloured, and everything was renewed, revived, refreshed, ready to greet the New Year, the spring. This year the earth was to give birth at the same time as Mahi, and she was overjoyed at the coincidence.

She was sure that the baby was going to be a girl. She had dreamt often about this and by the New Year she would have her second baby in her arms. She would be the image of herself, and Mahi dreamt how she was going to dress her, look after, cherish her. She was going to be the most beautiful girl, her girl, a part of herself. What a delight! She felt she was the happiest person on earth. She radiated joy and pleasure, her energy was limitless, she glowed with pleasure.

She was hoping for a birth on *Norooz* Day itself. She prayed that this would be so. Each time she prayed she ended with her wish, 'Oh Lord, make it possible for me to give birth on *Norooz* Day itself. This is my only ambition, please make it come true, grant me this one wish.'

'What a privilege giving birth at this time,' her friends told her, 'Everyone rejoicing your child's birth, and the whole of nature giving birth along with you.'

'What if it were to happen on *Norooz* Day itself?' The words came out before Mahi could control herself.

Khoshghadam looked at her with her big eyes, larger now, and they both were silent for a moment.

'That's an idea, Mahi, I never would have thought of it,' Koshghadam managed to utter, as they embraced.

'Imagine that!' both said at the same time, and they laughed.

Three days before *Norooz*, her brother Habib arrived with her *Norooz* presents as was the custom. Her family always sent a substantial pile of presents to her, even though she was now living far from home. She was delighted, she had been expecting this. She began to open the parcels, many of them in one big sack. There were sweets of many kinds, cakes, coloured eggs, tea, rice, oil, butter, cheese, henna and many other herbal preparations and delicacies and then, best of all, was a length of material, a beautiful brightly coloured piece to make

23

a dress. And she had a beautiful scarf as well.

'I thought Roghiieh would come with you,' Reza said to Habib that night. 'I think your sister will be giving birth any day now. I think she had better come straight away.'

Reza went back with Habib the next day to fetch Roghiieh and the day after they arrived together. It was New Year's Eve and Mahi had finished setting the *haftseen*. It was the ceremonial table. In the corner of the room she had spread an embroidered tablecloth, and on it she had arranged the traditional items. There were seven edible things, the names of which all started with 's'. There was *Sabzi*, the two plates of wheat and lentils she had sprouted, with a beautiful ribbon around them; *Somakh*, spice; *Senjed*, winter fruit; *Samanoo*, a special pudding made only around *Norooz*; *Sir*, garlic; and there was a goldfish in a bowl, a mirror, a candle and a *Koran*.

It looked stunning. The sight of it evoked a sense of tranquillity, the effect was uplifting. All the sweets and cakes and delicacies that she had prepared weeks in advance for *Norooz*, were there in a corner, not yet on display. They would be placed on another tablecloth, usually spread in the middle of the room, and put in different bowls or trays on *Norooz* Day itself and during the next two weeks for people to eat as they visited.

But now she was not sure how all this was going to be done as she was expecting to give birth any minute. She would leave that to her mother. Roghiieh would sort all that out, she had no need to worry, she said to herself.

Just after midnight, that *Norooz* Eve Mahi felt the labour begin. For a while she tried to lie still to let her mother, who was beside her on the roof, sleep, as she was tired after the journey. She tried to dream and forget the discomfort she was feeling but after a while she could not lie still. She started tossing and turning.

'Mahi, are you all right?' Roghiieh whispered.

'Yes, you go to sleep,' Mahi replied. 'You must be tired. I can't go to sleep, I'll go down for a bit, there are some things

I would like to do down there.'

'Do you think you are in labour?'

'I don't know, maybe.'

Both women sat up at the same time. Roghiieh held Mahi's hand in hers and for a few moments they sat in silence as though meditating together on the same thing.

'Let's go down, I'll come with you,' Roghiieh said, and they both climbed down the ladder.

Roghiieh woke up Reza, who was sleeping in the yard.

'Mahi's in labour,' she told him.

'Do you want me to go to fetch the midwife?' he asked.

'No, not now. I'll tell you when.'

Reza went up on to the roof, he would try to have a rest. Roghiieh would tell him when it was time to fetch the midwife.

Roghiieh made Mahi some herb tea. 'Come on, have a drink, this will do you good, it is Marjoram tea, it will help you along.'

After she had drunk her tea, Mahi said, 'I had better say my morning prayer.'

'Can you manage it?' Roghiieh asked.

'I think so, I'll try,' she replied.

'I'll do the same then,' Roghiieh said.

Then the two women went through the ablution, the ceremonial cleansing process before prayer. Mahi had difficulty in completing her prayer. It was very short, but for Mahi today it took a long time. Roghiieh did not interrupt her. 'She will stop if she can't manage,' she thought and busied herself with getting things ready, inspecting them again and making sure that everything was there.

Then the contractions began. By this time Khoshghadam had got up to say her prayer and had noticed the light next door. She realised what was happening and went straight to Mahi's house.

'Oh, this is wonderful, on the Day itself. Well done,

Mahi,' she cried with joy, hugging her. 'Shall I go and fetch the midwife?'

'No, you stay with me.' Mahi said. 'Reza can do that.'

Roghiieh went up on the roof, woke Reza and asked him to go and fetch the midwife. It was not long before the midwife arrived. Everything was ready, there was nothing for Mahi to worry about, her mother had come to take over, she would be doing the worrying from now on, she had handed over to her everything that was to be done. Everything was there. Baby clothes and equipment, herbal remedies, essential oils, Mahi was sure any help she needed would be given unconditionally by her mother, midwife, or her friends and her husband. She had all their support and the goodwill of the community. The only thing she had to do was to be concerned with the labour, 'ease into it', as women kept saying to her. She had heard it many times before.

'Just ease into it. Let the contractions just roll over you, don't resist, let things happen.'

Now the contractions were getting more frequent and longer. Women were shouting instructions at her.

'Now walk. Now squat. Now have a little drink. Just relax, you are doing fine.'

Soon Zahra, Khoshghadam's sister who had been staying with her came along as well. The women were laughing, joking, chatting, and Mahi laboured away in complete trust, comfort, peace of mind, totally happy. They kept massaging her, making her drinks, holding her as the contractions came.

'Just let your weight on to us, don't hold anything, we can take it,' and with each contraction the women relaxed totally into it.

With a few strong contractions, and the women telling her to push at the right moment, all of a sudden it was over, the baby was born, and a little girl!

That day, the twenty-first day of March, a double celebration was taking place in Mahi's house. *Norooz*, and the birth of her baby daughter. In her mind the whole world was celebrating with her.

Norooz

'But Mahi, give it a few days. Usually naming takes place three days after the birth.'

'No, I want it to be done today mother,' Mahi insisted. 'This is a very special day today, *Norooz* Day. She is born today and I want her to be named today.'

Roghiieh laughed. 'My dear Mahi, I won't argue with you, not today. You are stubborn, you have always been so.'

That very day the name-giving ceremony was performed when the house had been full with people, and Zuleha had whispered the name 'Monir' three times in the baby's ear.

'Now it is complete,' Mahi said to herself aloud. Only she knew exactly what that meant.

Later in the morning, soon after mother and baby had been settled, Roghiieh with the help of Khoshghadam and Zahra, started making the special kind of pancake which was made only for *Norooz*. Mahi had, as always, prepared the mixture the night before. It was a slow job and a special oil was used which made it extremely aromatic and very tasty. They had already made *kachee* for Mahi, a special food given to women around the time of childbirth. It was made out of rice flour with a special oil which was very rich but easy to digest and again, very aromatic.

Now, the *Norooz* festivity goodies had to be set out. Roghiieh spread out the large colourful table cloth, embroidered by Mahi, next to the *haftseen* corner. On it she set out many delicacies in beautiful bowls and plates, different kinds of sweets and nuts which Mahi had prepared weeks in advance. She arranged them beautifully, and with them she put a jug of rosewater.

Visitors started arriving – relatives, neighbours and friends. Roghiieh took the jug of rosewater around, sprinkling sparkling drops of water into each person's hand. The visitors rubbed it into their hands and onto their faces and said blessings and words of prayer. Then Mahi's mother offered them sweets and things to eat. Usually, the elders of the families would have been visited first, but this day, because Mahi had just given birth and Roghiieh was staying with her, everyone came to them, even Reza's older sister, Zolikha. Ali, resplendent from his bath the day before, was given a new shirt to put on and glowed with pleasure at all the attention and presents bestowed on him.

Throughout the day people were coming and going, they did not stay long but everyone popped in to bring New Year's greetings, together with greetings for the newborn. Even the men came, because this was a double celebration. Mahi relaxed happily, knowing that these festivities would carry on until the twelfth day of the New Year. She was particularly looking forward to the thirteenth day as that was a very special day, with its own ceremonial performances. Young women and children wore new, colourful clothes and the young women wore make-up. Khosh-ghadam had persuaded Mahi to wear a little make-up, so her eyes were made up with kohl, her finger and toe nails were coloured with henna.

Just before the New Year Mahi remembered how she had shaped her eyebrows by plucking, and had removed any facial hair. To remove her facial hair she had taken a piece of cotton, made a long loop, put it on her hands stretched out in front of her face and made the cotton into a triangular shape held with her fingers, with one end hooked on to something. By extending and tightening the loop using her fingers she had rubbed this gently across her face against the growth of the hair, to remove it, and simultaneously massage her skin. Mahi normally did this every few weeks, often together with Khoshghadam, as it was quicker and easier to manage with someone else. This New Year Mahi had made a special effort to look her best.

Mahi felt euphoric, on top of the world. She indulged herself in comfort, she was pampered, cherished, served by her mother, family, friends and the whole community. It seemed to her that the whole of nature rejoiced in her achievement. Today she was staying in bed, but was propped up from time to time, especially when the older people came in to greet her. When Zolikha, her sister-in-law arrived, Mahi tried to stand up as a sign of respect. 'No, no, don't get up,' Zolikha insisted, going towards her and giving her a hug. 'Well done, what a day for you, a double *Norooz*, and for us all.' And Mahi's face lit up.

The two women kissed each other on both cheeks and Zolikha took a look at the baby. 'God bless her, what a beautiful child.' She sat next to Mahi and the baby. Khoshghadam brought the rosewater to her and sprinkled it on her hands, then sweets were offered to her.

At this moment Roghiieh entered the room, greeting Zolikha, who in turn made a gesture to stand up out of respect, but Roghiieh motioned her to be seated as she went straight over. The two women kissed and hugged and then sat together to exchange a host of greetings, and questions about each other's health.

The day was spent entirely in entertaining visitors and it passed very quickly, as did the many days to come during which time Mahi did not concern herself with the routine chores of the house such as the cleaning and the cooking. The washing was done, the baby was cleaned, her little boy was looked after. She had handed over complete control of the house to her mother and her friends. She had total trust in them to look after her and her family and her only concern was herself. For ten days her mother stayed with her and cared for her and her family. During which time she did not need to worry about anything, just rest, enjoy and indulge. The house was never quiet now. People were always coming in to congratulate her, to celebrate with her the *Norooz*, the spring, the birth of her child, all intertwined into one. They also came to keep her company, to give practical help in the house, to be there because they believed that a woman who has just given birth should not be left alone, day or night. She was in a delicate and vulnerable state. She might be scared and so should have company at all times, especially that of other women.

The seventh day was the ceremonial cleansing day for Mahi. She was taken to the public bath house. Khosh-ghadam and Asli accompanied her and later Roghiieh took the baby to the bath where she was given a rinse while she waited, and then Mahi brought her home. The house was cleaned, aired, freshened for their return, and a big lunch was prepared for close relatives and a few friends. Delicacies were prepared and everyone had to have a taste of *kachee*.

After the seventh day the women of the neighbourhood came less often to the house. On the fortieth day, there was another ceremonial cleansing. Again Mahi was taken to the public bath house and her friends accompanied her. After a lengthy bath, the baby was also taken there as before, given a quick bath and returned home. Again a big lunch was prepared. This was to mark the end of her recovery period. From now on she was to take control of her life and look after her family. Roghiieh had already left, but there were older women nearby and Mahi knew that she could ask them for any help she needed, though she felt a lot more confident. This was her second child after all, she was experienced by now. She knew too that neighbours would pop in and give her a hand. They would do this automatically, just as she had done for them, no need for her to ask. This was as a matter of course in their relationship, expected of each other and done willingly. But Roghiieh would also keep close contact with her for some time to make sure everything was going all right.

From the moment of birth Monir slept in the same bed as her mother. So when Mahi slept she had the baby on one side and her little boy Ali on the other. Sometimes Ali went and slept with his father, which she encouraged him to do, especially since the baby's arrival. Sometimes the bedding was arranged in such a way that Mahi would lie first, next to her the baby, then Ali and finally Reza, they would sleep all in a row. And sometimes it would be Mahi on one side of the baby, on the other Ali, and next to Ali Reza would sleep. Whatever the arrangement the baby would always be next to Mahi, next to her body. In the night when the baby woke up Mahi would put her breast in the baby's mouth, sometimes in her sleep without properly waking up, and she would suckle then fall asleep again, both in complete comfort. The baby had to sleep close to her mother's body. How could it be otherwise, they had been flesh to flesh for nine months. So Mahi would keep this contact for a few years to come. She saw it as a crucial part of the baby's growth, and they had this bodily closeness for many years to come.

The baby rarely cried in the day or at night. In the night she woke up and made just enough noise to alert Mahi to put the nipple in her mouth. She slept warm and secure in her warm, damp, tightly packed nappies. She was changed once in the morning, once in the afternoon and the last time in the evening. At night, she stayed comfortingly wrapped, as if in the womb.

At times, Mahi worked around the house, with the baby strapped to her back or front. Always the baby was close to her. Sometimes Mahi would swing her to sleep in a hammock which had been slung by a rope from the ceiling, in a corner of the main living area. Whenever there was a problem, Mahi knew she could call on her mother-in-law or the older women. They had herbal remedies if the baby should be ill, and essential oils for massage and inhalation. Mahi and the baby both felt secure. Mahi had a favourite way to put her baby to sleep, which was to sit down on the floor, with her legs stretched out in front, a cushion placed on her feet and a little mat on her legs, with the baby resting safely on it. Then she would gradually rock her legs until the baby drifted off to sleep. Then gently she would pull her legs out and leave the baby to sleep on the floor.

In the summer when families slept either on the roof or in the garden, Mahi would take out the bedding so that the whole family could sleep in a row. The younger children were kept closer to the mother, the older closer to the father, so Mahi slept with Monir, Ali with Reza, all in a row. In winter, they slept inside around the *korsi*, a very large stool, covered with a big eiderdown, which was placed over the *tanoor*, a fireplace made out of clay, dug into the ground, which was used for baking bread in the morning, when a new fire was lit, and for slow cooking throughout the day. The mother and baby slept at one side, Ali on Mahi's other side, and Reza at the far end. And in autumn and spring when the *korsi* was not around they would sleep in the room, again all in a row. If cousins, nephews and neices visited they just extended the bedding, all sleeping together except for the men who had separate beds.

Soon after Monir was born a line was drawn all around the wall, to keep out evil and protect the baby. Whenever she was handled – to be changed, washed or fed, a blessing was said, such as 'In the name of God'. After all, it was believed the child was a gift from God, the feelings of sanctity must be expressed!

Monir had half a dozen triangular nappies, all of different sizes, and each made up of layers of fine cotton sewn quilt-like together. She was tightly wrapped up in these so that she would not feel too different from being in the womb. She had been tightly packed inside the mother for nine months, and any change must be gradual. Her whole body, right up to the neck, was wrapped in this way with a string all around the middle, keeping her tight. Gradually, over the months, Mahi left less of the body inside the wraps. First the arms would be left out, then more of the body, until at the age of nine months just the bottom would be left inside.

So Mahi and Monir were very close. Neighbours and relatives looked after Ali, so that they could be together as much as possible, and so that Mahi could rest, enjoy her baby and keep her energy for the newborn. They still helped her with the housework, cooking and other chores, and Roghiieh was, of course, Mahi's first source of support. The two women talked intimately, about everything. Mahi shared with Roghiieh all her problems and her joys, her pains, her worries, her experiences with her in-laws, husband or neighbours, anything she experienced or did not like or understand, all were discussed with her mother. After a visit to her she felt cleaned, cleared, inwardly renewed and came back refreshed, energised, wiser. A woman's strength came from her mother.

Mahi enjoyed breastfeeding her baby, she loved those moments. Sitting down cross-legged on the floor, leaning on some cushions against the wall, holding her baby in her arms, putting her to her breasts, she loved the flow of milk from her breast to her baby, the process gave her a sensual pleasure. The suckling made her feel good, she felt the flow of the milk, this life-giving substance, was a transfer of life energy from her to her baby.

Mahi admired the baby as she suckled vigorously and swallowed the rush of milk which squirted out with each suck, much more than her mouth and throat could cope with. She stroked her, cuddled her, talked to her and whispered endearments. The baby lapped up all the milk and the admiration, she was saturated in it, swamped by it. She soaked it all up, as if to take from it enough sustenance for a lifetime. The sense of ecstasy flowed over her, as she dipped into it with greed she was enriched, contented. Her world was made up of the milk and the love which her mother gave unconditionally.

Mahi spoke gently to her, 'My little angel, my beautiful angel, your mother will be sacrificed to you, my dearest, my life, my beauty.' She laughed with her, they smiled at each other, responded to each other, they looked in each other's eyes, in each other's hearts, connecting with each other's soul.

Mahi's breasts filled as quickly as they were emptied. She had more than enough milk. She could have fed ten babies, she remarked to Khoshghadam laughingly. She fed Hajar's baby girl, when her friend, who had been unwell for some time, was too weak to feed her own child at the breast. Hajar's baby would be brought to Mahi and she would either feed them, sometimes her own first, and then the other, or at times for the fun of, it she would put both babies to her breasts at the same time and watch them with amazement, pleasure and curiosity as to how they were doing, and then would focus on her own feelings. Now on her feelings, now on theirs.

It was a challenge feeding two babies at the same time, caring for them, coping with their needs and experiencing the pleasure in them which in turn gave her pleasure. She loved these moments. She enjoyed them immensely. Then she would play with them for a bit, watching their expressions, smiles and satisfaction on their faces, as though seeing their growth, experiencing it. Through breastfeeding Hajar's daughter, Mahi had a very special relationship with her, and often called her 'my milk-daughter' and told her children that this was their 'milk-sister'.

Mahi was not the only woman to feed another woman's baby. It happened often. If a mother was severely ill, the baby sometimes would be fed by the grandmother, the baby's sucking bringing milk back into the older woman's breast. In fact, just as Mahi was feeding her friend's baby, her mother began feeding Khadijeh, her eldest daughter's child. Khadijeh was very depressed after being divorced by her husband, so Roghiieh took the baby to feed.

Breastmilk was life-giving, considered sacred, a substance which put humanity into people. It gave human dignity. To say that someone had not had mother's milk implied that they had behaved very badly. Anyone with a taste of mother's milk would not be capable of behaving in such a way. 'I will not bless my milk in you,' Mahi would sometimes hear an angry mother say to another adult. 'Your mother's milk to be halal, blessed in you.' 'Let the goodness of your mother's milk no longer be with you.' Without mother's milk, one could not possibly have goodness inside. And so Mahi fed her daughter with great pleasure and glory, something she continued to do for each of her children, until they were nearly two years old.

It was at this time that Hajar lost her baby after a lengthy illness. Smallpox was sweeping away many lives in Kahleh and the surrounding villages. Hajar was distraught. A funeral was held, and the women in the neighbourhood gathered at Hajar's house. They all cried with her. Mahi was particularly distressed, to have lost her milk-child like this. The women sat around her as Hajar cried loudly, calling out at times: 'My dearest one, how young you died, how little time I had you to myself, how short your life was.' With each sentence she uttered they echoed her cries, they listened to her and their voices rose, to be lowered again to listen to the next lament. At times she would hit herself on the head. She sat there for hours in the middle of all the women, all crying together. Then Mahi put the samovar on to soft boil an egg, which she broke, stirred, and then gave to Hajar and told her to drink it up. She kept insisting until she had drunk it all. And then Khoshghadam made some sweetened tea for her, stirred it and gave it to her, insisting that she should drink it. And then everyone else had a drink.

All that day, people visited Hajar, so that she was always in company, and was not left alone for a minute. They offered her food occasionally and insisted that she should take it, and gave her drinks with honey. But they allowed her to grieve and they shared her grief with her.

In the evening Mahi and Khoshghadam prepared a meal for her family and brought it in. They all ate together and the women stayed with her late into the night. Hajar's sister stayed with her overnight in case she should need anything and as company if she could not sleep.

For the next seven days Hajar was surrounded by people. All her chores were done by other women so that she could grieve the death of her baby in full without having to deal with other everyday concerns. Meanwhile, Mahi felt very anxious about her own children's health. It was not long before Mahi's little daughter also had smallpox. Mahi felt angry, powerless. The disease quickly got a grip on Monir and soon she was severely ill. Mahi was very alarmed. Her worst fear was that she might lose her daughter. She embarked on a series of rituals for her recovery, having first bandaged her daughter's eyes. First, she took an egg and sat near the child and named people whom she suspected of having cast an evil eye on her. With each name she tapped on the egg. The name at which the egg broke would be the person who had given the evil eye. With this performance she hoped the danger would pass. Then she put some *esfand*, a herb, on the fire so that the smoke from it would cleanse away the evil.

After a day or two, when the illness did not subside, she put a coin under her pillow overnight, a coin which she had managed to save for a rainy day. This was indeed a rainy day. The next morning she circled it round the little girl's head and then gave it away as alms. This she hoped would make the illness subside.

Mahi took candles to the mosque, and made a vow to visit the local shrine, which was some distance away, when Monir was well enough. She consulted the village healer, donated grain to the mosque and planned a sacrifice of her only valuable possession, her wedding ring, at the shrine of Saint Zinab. But nothing seemed to work, and Monir showed no sign of improvement. Mahi felt utterly helpless, and did not know what more she could do to save her daughter. Night after night Mahi sat next to her little daughter's body as the burning fire raged in her, as her fiery breath came faster, throughout the grim, long winter nights, as the snow lay heavy outside and covered their house. Inside lay Monir, hot like a bowl of fire. Mahi would not close her eyes for a minute, but just sat there holding her daughter's hand listening to her quick, shallow breathing and her heartbeat. She prayed, she wept. Praying and weeping, that was all she could do.

Monir's illness lasted for three months. Three long, grey, hard, winter months. The little girl had pulled through but only just. By the end of her illness she was skin and bone. Finally Mahi took the bandages off her eyes and it was then she discovered that her daughter had lost her sight. Mahi was devastated. For a long time Mahi felt her world had ended, she felt she had lost her daughter. But her family and friends, and the whole village, offered support and consolation, and gave every help possible. Zolikha especially was a great comfort, often taking Monir to her house and looking after her for several days, to give Mahi a break. This eased her distress but could not make up for the sense of loss she felt.

Khoshghadam

Khoshghadam was Mahi's closest friend in the village.
Mahi often thought back to their first meeting on the eve
of her wedding day, shortly after her arrival from Khorbendeh.

'This is your next-door neighbour, Khoshghadam,' Aunt
Zolikha had said, as she put Khoshghadam's hand into
Mahi's.

'May your arrival be a happy one like mine,' Khoshghadam whispered in her ear. 'Cheer up, let's see a bridal
look on your face.' And the two women had laughed.

'That's better,' Khoshghadam and Aunt Zolikha had said
together. It was the first time Mahi had laughed that day.

Her mood changed instantly, she felt happy, light.
Khoshghadam's presence gave her a sense of security,
assurance. They looked into each other's eyes. Yes, she
could trust her. They were holding hands. 'I must make
room for the bridegroom,' her new friend said, laughingly.
Mahi held her hand tighter, they had clicked instantly.
They stayed together chatting, whispering, joking, until it
was time for Mahi to be taken in with her bridegroom for
her wifely duty. She could not let go of Khoshghadam's
hand easily.

'You'll see her tomorrow morning,' Aunt Zolikha had said, gently pulling her away.

'I'll be round to see you in the morning, I promise,' Khoshghadam whispered, and pulled her hand off and slipped away. With Aunt Zolikha one side and Roghiieh on the other, holding her arms, they walked her into the bride's bedroom, where her husband awaited her. The next morning, the first thing she asked her mother was where was Khoshghadam. She was over within minutes. The two women were left alone for a while. They talked, not about what went on the night before. The two women talked and giggled.

Roghiieh had stayed for three days, and every day Hushkadam popped in two or three times. Now Mahi was looking forward to her mother leaving, then she would be able to spend more time with Khoshghadam. On the day Roghiieh left Mahi went to her friend's house. They spent a whole day together chatting as they worked, first they did Khoshghadam's housework and then Mahi's.

Then a few days later Khoshghadam gave a party, a special soup party. She invited six friends, to introduce them to Mahi so they could get to know her and cheer her up. There was Sedigheh, newly married and expecting her first child; Mahin, with one child; Batoo, newly married who was also expecting; Zahra, with a baby boy in her arms; Safieh and Tahereh, two sisters from the next village who had just married two brothers in Kahleh. All the women were in their mid or late teens. Khoshghadam told Mahi a bit about each of them, so that she would feel as if she knew them a little before they arrived.

Mahi helped her to make the *ash reshteh*, the special soup for these big gatherings, made from chick peas, green lentils, kidney beans, beetroot leaves, freshly cut spaghetti-style pasta, fried onions, mint and garlic flavoured with *kashk*, a dried, reconstituted yoghurt. The women ate together, talked, laughed, joked, danced, played hide-and-seek, dressed up, some in men's clothes, it was very theatrical. Mahi was thrilled about the party. It was the most enjoyable day she had spent since her own wedding day.

From then on Mahi and Khoshghadam spent most of their time together and their friendship grew rapidly. Khoshghadam was a few years older than Mahi. She was eighteen and Mahi was fifteen. She had one child, a girl aged two. She was a big woman, tall and heavily built, with a mischievous face and large, black, penetrating eyes which saw right through you and laughed all the time. Mahi soon learnt that she was known as the 'Laughing Eyes Girl' in the village, and also that Khoshghadam was a gypsy, who had fallen in love with and married Ahmad, then settled in Kahleh despite her family's disapproval who wanted her to marry another gypsy. 'I'll find my own husband in time,' she had always said. And indeed, she had found him eventually. One day while they were helping with each other's housework, Khoshghadam had told Mahi the story of how they met.

'I met Ahmad when we were passing through this very village, Kahleh, at a harvest festival. I was just fourteen at the time. My mother had been reading Ahmad's palm and I was dancing in a group of dancers.'

'How old was Ahmad?' asked Mahi.

'He must have been about sixteen. My mother had told him, "Your future wife is very close, I can smell her. Funnily enough it is a familiar smell to me." Then she looked into the distance, and for a moment she fell silent. "Well, what will be, will be." She had come suddenly to herself, so Ahmad tells me. "That's enough for you." She stopped the palm reading abruptly. Many youngsters had gathered around her waiting for their palms to be read, but she refused to continue with the readings. "That's enough for the day," she said, "off you go, all of you." Meanwhile Ahmad had joined in with the dancing and so that is how we met. We danced and talked and later that evening we looked into each other's eyes and knew we had both fallen hopelessly in love. I sensed at that moment that I had found my future husband,' Khoshghadam had told Mahi. 'I made a vow that I would marry no one but this man, and I told him so.'

'But my family wouldn't accept it, so in the end Ahmad and I had no choice but to run away together.'

'But weren't you worried about their anger, the shame you would bring on the family?' Mahi gasped.

'I knew they would come around eventually, as indeed they did. And as for shame – what shame? After all, who can change their fate . . . my mother saw it all in Ahmad's hand!' said Khoshghadam, gently laughing. 'And remember, Mahi, don't get too close to your in-laws, they will have a hold on you, keep your distance. It is better this way, then the relationship will not get sour when you want to assert your independence.' Mahi and Khoshghadam shared many secrets about their past lives, their loves, hopes and fears. They became inseparable and were known as each other's shadow. 'Where is your shadow, Mahi? I can't see her. Oh there she is,' friends would tease her. Khoshghadam looked after her like a younger sister, especially when Reza was away. 'There is a lot for you to learn, Mahi,' she would say. She showed her how to carry heavy loads. They would gather firewood and chop logs, and go mountain walking and rock climbing together. They went for long walks in the fields and the hills gathering herbs and roots and flowers for healing. Khoshghadam was an expert in herbs, roots and plants, and she taught Mahi all she knew about their properties. 'You have to learn to survive in difficult conditions as we gypsies do. Life here in the village is very easy, people are lazy, they don't know what hard work is. Look at these rocks, see how strong, firm and majestic they are. People are like that too, it is just that we have to discover and realise our strength and use it. Be strong and tough like the rock.'

When Reza was away the two women spent most of their time together. They would sit together late into the

42

night, chatting as they worked with their hands, knitting, sewing, embroidering, mending or spinning wool. Eventually Mahi would say, 'Sleep here tonight, it is too late to go home now, soon it will be morning.' Khoshghadam sometimes stayed, running home early in the morning to attend to her child.

'Life is not only about men, you know,' Khoshghadam once said during one of their evenings together. 'There is a lot more to life than just having a man to stand by you. We see so little of them, and when we do it is mainly in the night. It is then that we have to perform our little wifely duty. Let them have it, give them what they need, it will only take a few moments. Then go and enjoy it properly with the person of your own choice.'

'You are dreadful, Khoshghadam. I'll tell your husband, you just wait.'

'Tell him if you dare, you will be seen as being as bad as me! Can you imagine your husband's face, knowing you have been with me all this time?'

The two women roared with laughter, hugging each other.

Landlords

Tales of wicked landlords were legion. The landlord in Mahi's village was called Iadollahkhan (Iad – arm, ollah – God, khan – master, the master arm of God). 'The Arm of God, he is the arm of the devil himself,' Mahi said one day in conversation with Khoshghadam. They often talked about him, his heartlessness, his cruelty and inhumanity.

They both recalled the time that a story was going round that the *arbab* (the landlord) was selling and sending abroad the hundreds of carpets that women had been making in his many villages. Khoshghadam had heard with her own ears from her friend Hamideh's mother who had worked in the *arbab's* house briefly as a maid, she had seen it, she knew it. She said that they were all sent by flying machines which went through the sky very fast like birds. Mahi had heard about these flying machines. Apparently they all went to Teheran, although this she had not heard directly, no one in the village had, only through the people who had been in Teheran. A few people from the village had been to the capital briefly, they had heard them, seen them in the sky. Hamideh had said that piles of the carpets were taken on horseback to Hamadan, the nearest town, from there by lorry to Teheran and from Teheran these flying birds took them off to foreign countries. She could not remember the names but they were very far away. In these countries the rich people, and they were all rich over there, furnished their houses with these beautiful carpets. The *arbab* got a lot of money for them.

Mahi had remembered all the carpets she had made for him, how much of herself she had put into them, especially the most recent one, that she had finished last winter. She took it to him the very evening she completed it, hoping for good payment. She had done all the work for that carpet herself, starting from scratch. She had looked after the goats, eight of them, and their babies. She had sheared them, washed the wool and dried it in the sun and then fluffed it by hand, bit by bit, with patience and care. Then she had spun it and made the wool into loops ready for dying, each loop stretching about half a metre in diameter and weighing about half a kilo. After dying the wool she then undid the loops and made them into balls. Then she used them to weave the carpet, stitch by stitch, through many long nights under a weak paraffin lamp, keeping the filter down to save paraffin. Her eyes and fingers had ached but she forced herself to keep going night after night. She had worked on it day and night for three months.

At the end of it, the day she cut it down, it was a beauty. Everyone admired it, especially Aunt Zolikha, who said it was the best work she had seen yet. Mahi couldn't believe her ears, coming from Aunt Zolikha, that was something, she had not dreamt of hearing those words from her. She had hugged Mahi and kissed her on both cheeks, 'You clever girl, this is a beauty, a masterpiece.' She had been over the moon with all this praise. Mahi had created a new pattern on that carpet, flowers and birds, butterflies and blossoms, branches and leaves, bushes and grass, mountains and candles. It was magical, the colours exquisite, the way she had combined them all. 'It is breathtaking,' Aunt Zolikha said.

'It's like a dream,' added Khoshghadam.

45

It was her dream, for she had indeed woven all her dreams and desires into that carpet, and her joys and sorrows, into its colours and patterns.

Mahi had been inspired by various events and emotions, as she wove the carpet. After the death of her great uncle the pattern emerged of a swallow leaving behind a hilly, barren, rocky village and flying into a warm, green, fertile faraway land. And for lovemaking Mahi showed a pair of butterflies in petals and leaves, who had reached a state of absolute ecstasy.

She wove in beauty and perfection with the stitches, one by one. Now she could see it was a mirror, her mirror. All this had come out of her, it was part of her. She felt proud of it.

The evening when Mahi had taken the carpet to the landlord's house, he had walked on it, up and down, kept admiring it. 'But this is a beauty, the best amongst my carpets yet. The design is unique. So different from all the other ones. It is very special. I think I will keep this one. Who made it?' He had addressed his assistant.

'That one over there,' he had pointed her out.

'Oh, that woman, yes. Give her a few kilos of barley, yes, make it five,' he had mumbled. Mahi had just heard it. She was eagerly waiting for his verdict, for his reward. His verdict was all right. He could not stop admiring it. 'The best amongst my carpets yet.' That was really a compliment, coming from him. But the reward. She was devastated.

'Only five kilos of barley, not even wheat, heartless man. Was that all that he could give me? Was that all that it was worth? After I had put so much of myself into it, was that all he was rewarding me, five kilos of barley?' She could not repeat it often enough. 'My life had gone into that, and my family's, I even ignored my family's needs, and put all my energy into that carpet for three months, day and night. My fingers and eyes are still burning, my heart is burning, I strapped my sick baby on my back as I worked away. That man has no humanity in him, he has a heart of stone. After all that praise, that was all he gave me, that's all he thought I deserved.' The injustice of it all set her heart aflame once again as she thought of it, she raged with anger. 'Only a man is capable of such atrocities,' she said inwardly.

Each house in the village made one or two carpets a year. 'He has got hundreds of villages, they say, imagine thousands of carpets being made for him every year, what does he do with all these carpets? He should be able to carpet the whole land as far as the human eye can see, imagine that?' Zahra had once remarked.

Iadollahkhan's desire for wealth and power was boundless. He terrorised the villages. He had a foul temper when it flared up, and it did not take much to anger him, he gave no mercy. He had hacked two men, Hussein and Hojat, to death in the village square in public, to teach everyone else a lesson. 'You useless lot, you produce nothing, you deserve nothing, it is a waste of land having you as tenants and yet you expect a return. What have you produced to expect a return?' he had said on one occasion.

'But sir, we do our best,' Hussein had dared to voice.

He had jumped at him there and then, with a knife, right into his stomach, and he had circled the knife round to enlarge the hole. 'You dare to answer back, this will keep you quiet, you little worm, and your useless friends.' His friends had taken his body to his home. It was said that some of his innards had fallen out, which they had picked up and pushed back inside his stomach. 'Foolish man, he should not have spoken,' some of the older men had said. 'He spoke for all of us, I wish more of us would dare to do it,' voiced one young man. The body had lain for three days in his home and peasants had come from miles around the village to pay him respect for his courage in having spoken out for all of them. After three days they gave him a hero's burial.

Hojat's sin had been to protest against his bride being taken away from him on his wedding night. Hojat and

Majan had been childhood sweethearts. The landlord had heard about Majan, a girl of striking beauty and intelligence, from his assistants, or so the story went. Those who served him in this way were known as his 'eyes and ears', just as the King himself had 'eyes and ears'. Hearing that she was about to be married off he had decided to have her that very night before her husband, so when the house had been emptied from guests, his men had gone in to take her.

Hojat had resisted violently, but after a struggle he had been knocked out and Majan had been carried away by force. When he came around he had screamed all night, wanting to get out and get at the landlord, but he was held back. Majan had been released in the village late that night after being raped and she had thrown herself into a disused well. They found her the next day, but she never regained consciousness. That very same day Hojat had run out of the house, found his way to the master's house and spat in his face. He was captured, tied up and taken to the village square where everyone was called to witness his punishment. The time had been set to coincide with the midday call to prayer, no one turned up, except the priest who had gone, in vain, to ask for mercy for Hojat's family. The landlord himself had stabbed the man many times over and then ordered the body to be hung in the square for three days for everyone to see. His men made sure that this was done, guarding the body for three days so that no one dared to take it down.

And then there was the tale of Hassan Ali. He had been the village shepherd for as long as anyone could remember. No one knew his exact age but it was thought that he was nearly a hundred years old. He had been a shepherd from the age of eight, accompanying his father who had in turn taken over from his father. This job had been in his family for generations, passing from father to son. He had only given it up when his eyesight finally failed and he became hard of hearing. He had had poor eyesight for quite a long time and it was said that he controlled the herd with his voice but also by playing the flute. Depending on the tune he played the animals knew what to do and responded. There was a particular tune to which all the animals would gather and lie down for their afternoon rest. He would play a special tune in the evening after giving three long calls. The animals would come running from every direction when they heard his call and the tune, then he would set off for the village. It was said that he talked to the animals, praised them, admired them for being productive, giving, and for being good-tempered.

Hassan Ali's back was bent, and people had enormous respect for his age and experience. One early morning he had been waiting in the village square for the grocery shop to open to get his tobacco. Some children had been playing nearby. Suddenly there was dust on the horizon and a horse appeared over the hill galloping towards the village. The children ran away, shouting, 'The Master, the Master.' The horse approached the square and stopped where Hassan Ali was sitting. A rider jumped off, 'Stand up, you old man,' he shouted. Hassan Ali was surprised at this sudden command and tried to stand up, but he was slow. 'You can do it quicker than that, you stupid old man.' Hassan Ali managed to stand up, but he was shaky. 'Look at me,' the man shouted, 'who am I?' Hassan Ali had understood by now who this man was, only Iadollahkhan would treat him in this manner.

'Yes, sir, you are the Master, Iadollahkhan himself.'

'So why didn't you stand up in time and greet me as I approached?' he said loudly. Then, before Hassan Ali could explain, he ordered his two men, who had just reached them and were getting off their horses, that this man should receive twenty lashes, in this very square, for having ignored his approach. There should be a public call to witness his punishment so that everyone would learn a lesson from it.

On that very morning, Hassan Ali was flogged. 'But I am

blind, sir, I did not recognise you on your arrival,' he shouted as he was dragged to the middle of the square.

'That's a good excuse,' Iadollahkhan laughed, 'carry on with your orders,' he commanded. In his presence every-one had to stand up, then bow to him, and remain standing until he was out of sight. Twenty lashes were admin-istered. The old man lost consciousness. Some people watched from their rooftops.

Hassan Ali never regained consciousness, three days later he passed away.

Unlike some other landlords, Iadollahkhan did not allow movements from his land, so no one dared to leave. People could come on to his land, if they wished, but this never happened because of the tales of his atrocities and terror. Early death was common amongst his tenants. Mahi remarked that only a man could possess such a degree of evil. 'But his wife is no better,' Khoshghadam reminded her. Iadollahkhan had been married three times, and had many children – no one knew how many. And he would regularly rape young women who had been taken by force from their homes. There had been many cases of a pregnant maid being 'sacked' by his wife. She would put them in a sack, tie it up and then stab them all over with a large needle and then leave them to die in their own blood. Goli had been one such victim.

Goli wasn't even thirteen when she was taken by force to Iadollahkan's house to work as a maid for his wife. Her mother, Ashraf, was the midwife in the village and was very much loved and respected. She'd cried bitterly and pleaded with the madam, 'Have mercy on her and don't let her get hurt.'

'You should be grateful, woman, that your daughter will live in my house and relieve you of feeding and clothing her,' she'd said, 'And now go, and don't try to come and see her. This would only disturb her, unsettle her. Let her settle down, for a year anyway, and then I'll let you know when to come and visit her.' With that she'd ordered her to leave.

Eight months had passed, and Ashraf had only received news of her, that she was fine, but had not seen her daughter. Then one Friday, she had a message to go and collect her daughter's body. 'I knew something dreadful would happen that day. I had a dream in the night and I was waiting for it.'

Nana Soghra, an old woman who had lived almost all her life in the landlord's household, told the story, 'Well, it was yesterday morning. I heard shouting, screams and Madam calling for me. Goli was crying painfully, hugging her stomach, she must have kicked her in the stomach. "Nana Soghra, did you know this girl's tummy has come up?"

"No Madam," I said, "Are you sure?"

"I'm sure," she was shouting, "Well, it is true and I want her to tell me who has done it. Do you have any ideas?"

"No Madam," I replied. I knew instantly who was responsible for this.

"I'll get it out of her. Tell Cheraghali to cut a few branches. Take the leaves off and bring them to me. Hurry!"

I left the room. I was trembling. Her manservant, Cheraghali, had already heard her request. She dipped the branches in the pool. They were hefty ones. She ordered Goli to take her clothes off. She tore them off her as she kicked her about, and then with the wet branches she whipped her as hard as she could. "Who did it? Who? Tell me who!" she shouted with each whip. Each time a branch broke she took another one. She kicked her, punched her, dragged her about by her hair. Goli was screaming, pleading, calling for her mother. "Who?" she kept shouting. "*Arbab*, my lord," Goli blurted out, and with it she passed out.

"Daub and a match," the Madam shouted. She poured water over her and held smoking daub under her nose. Goli came round. "A large sack, Nana Soghra," she demanded. I could not move, as if nailed down, I knew what this meant. "Are you deaf, woman!" she shouted. "Cheraghali, a large sack!" she shouted, "Hurry, and string." She took the sack, put it over Goli's head, pushed her inside it, tied it with string, then brought two large needles, holding one in each hand. She pricked her through, frantically, all around. Soon the blood was pouring out. "This'll teach you, and your type, you little worm!" The screams of that girl shook the earth, filled the sky, reached the stars. There can't be a God I said to myself. She continued this attack for quite some time after Goli had stopped screaming. She was still doing it when I left the room. I had to rush to the toilet. I vomited, and passed out. "Give that body to her mother to be shown in the village square, for the likes of her to learn a lesson."'

'Since she could not confront her husband about his acts, she punished the women for his crimes, when the *arbab* is the one who ought to be punished,' Khoshghadam commented.

Many were the times Mahi and Khoshghadam spoke of their dreams for the future, of a life away from the landlord's tyranny. 'One day I will leave, I swear I will,' Mahi insisted, ignoring her friend's incredulous smile, 'You just wait and see!'

Storytelling

On long winter nights people would visit each other for company and entertainment. These get-togethers were called 'Night Sittings'. Two or three times a week a big gathering of ten to fifteen people would meet, babies and children included. Sometimes the gatherings were arranged or sometimes people just dropped by. They would start early, after the evening meal, and would go on until midnight.

It was at these gatherings that great storytelling took place. Myths, fairy tales, historical events, events and experiences from faraway lands, and family histories were all told. As they listened the women did knitting, sewing, patchwork or embroidery. Old and young, men and women, children and babies were all there.

Mahi loved these Night Sittings and storytelling. When it was held at her house she called upon Aunt Zolikha or her great uncle to come and tell stories, they were both so good at it. As older people they had the experience, the knowledge, and the wisdom for storytelling. One night this great uncle of Mahi, who had been visiting them, was asked to tell a story. When Great Uncle and Aunt Zolikha entered the room that evening the people gathered in the

53

room stood up as a sign of respect and waited until they were seated, before sitting down themselves. Great Uncle was greeted first, people bowed to him and younger men took their hats off for him.

Mahi had a houseful that night with family, friends, and neighbours; with children and babies who either slept or listened to the rhythmic voice of the great uncle which at times became quite excited. People sat around the *korsi*, Great Uncle sat at its head and after the preliminary conversations the storytelling began. The water pipe was prepared and put in front of him on the *korsi* and drinks were prepared for everyone else. He told the story of the hidden treasure; how Mahi's grandfather had a fortune buried in the grounds of his house. The story went like this:

Her grandfather, who had been a wealthy man, had two sons. The older son, Ahmad, who was to become Mahi's father, had been flamboyant as a youngster, meddling in gambling, drinking, drug-taking, and womanising. Whereas the younger one, Hamid, a deep-thinking type, had been involved in politics and eventually was to be killed in the Kurdish Liberation Army during the war with the government troops.

The grandfather who did not want his wealth to be gambled away by Ahmad thought of a solution, on the thirteenth day of the New Year. On this national festival day people take to the hills and the fields for the day, to celebrate the coming of the spring and the fertility of the earth, the rebirth and renewal of nature. Everyone did this to get rid of all their worries and concerns of the old year and welcome the good and the wellbeing of the new year into their lives. They took barbecues, lots of fruit, sweets and delicacies to eat, and tambourines. Extended families, grandparents, aunts, uncles, nieces, nephews, cousins, children and babies, the lot, picnicked at the sides of streams, rivers and springs and walked the hills, fields, meadows and orchards. Women played their tambourines and clapped and danced as they moved to the music, making their way from hill to hill. They cupped their hands to drink water which rushed from the hills over the stones down to the valleys. They danced, they sang, they laughed, they played, they rejoiced with nature, the fertility, the abundance of the spring, of the new year, which filled the air around them.

That day the grandfather decided to stay behind in the house all on his own, he had business to attend to. After the family left, he dismissed the only servant who had stayed behind to look after him, 'You go with your family to the festival, I'll be all right,' he said. The servant, a curious young man, decided to stay hidden in the house to find out what the master was up to. The house, set in large grounds, comprised in effect two houses, an interior one for women and children, and around that a larger area which contained the main house for the menfolk, a servants' quarter and a compound where the animals were kept.

The servant, having said goodbye to his master, made his way to the far end of the garden where he climbed a tall tree to get a good view over the house, hiding himself among the branches. He watched as his master spent a long while sitting in the garden in the sun, puffing away on his water pipe. It was as if he was in a trance, so much so that the servant worried about him, whether he was alright, alive even. Just as he decided to go and investigate he noticed movements, and the next thing he saw to his astonishment, was that the master was digging just behind his living quarters. He could not understand for the life of him why his master should be digging the ground on his own. Then he saw his master lifting something, but from so far away and that height he could not see the details. He made his way down from the tree and got as near as he could to the house where he climbed a tree there to see exactly what was going on.

It was an extraordinary sight. A large hole had been dug

in the ground, with a great pile of earth next to it on one side, and on the other side there stood three large earthenware pots, each about a metre in height and about half a metre in diameter. The old man had a bucket of water, a bowl of salt, and three pieces of cloth spread out next to each other in the sunshine. He was taking a handful of coins out of each pot, dipping them into the water, coating them with salt, rubbing them in his hand and throwing them onto one of the cloths. Three separate piles. One pile was gold coins, one silver, and the third bronze coins. He took a handful of coins at a time, moving from gold to silver and then to bronze, then started again with gold. The piles were getting bigger and bigger. 'I was mesmerised. I kept rubbing my eyes and pinching myself to make sure I wasn't dreaming,' the servant would recount years later. No, it wasn't a dream, it was real, it was actually happening, the piles were getting bigger by the minute. The pots seemed to have been filled with them. 'I was beyond myself with excitement, I couldn't believe my eyes. Unfortunately a sudden sneeze seized me and before I was able to do anything about it, out it came, a great big sneeze. He looked up and saw me. I was in disgrace. At that moment I wished the ground would open up and swallow me. He was cursing me now. He threw a handful of silver coins towards me and said, 'Take it and be gone, not a word to anyone, do you understand?' Somehow I managed to pick the coins up and just ran.'

He kept his promise, the servant, not a word to anyone until the grandfather had gone, only then did the story come out and the search began for the coins. First the original spot was dug up and thoroughly searched. Nothing was found. It was obvious that he had not put the coins back there. Since then the land has been dug up all over, some spots many times over, but no sign of the coins has ever been found. It is believed that the treasure must have moved, as earthquakes were commonplace in that part of the country and where it has moved to no one knows.

Mahi's great uncle told many anecdotes, recited poetry, recounted stories and experiences from faraway villages and towns, from past history. The water bobbler was passed around occasionally for people to have a puff or two which made it gurgle and bubble as he brought to life the stories he told. Everyone was spellbound as he added his own moral points and jokes. His age, knowledge and wisdom were held in high esteem. He was looked after and served with dedication, he was highly valued and people showed him deep respect. Aunt Zolikha was held in similar high esteem. Her blessing was asked at times of major changes such as at a wedding, birth, or death. When her younger sister, Asli got married, her consent was asked for as older sister. It was thought that Aunt Zolikha had healing powers, at times of illness she would be asked to come and lay hands. Her visit alone would be considered as having a healing effect. That evening when Great Uncle had finished his tale, Mahi begged Zolikha to tell one of her stories. At first Aunt Zolikha said she was too tired but finally she gave in to Mahi's pleas and began:

There was one, there was no one, except God, there was no one.

There was a Queen who longed to have a child, but she could not conceive. One day she made a vow, 'If I have a child, I shall give eight kilogrammes of honey and eight kilogrammes of oil to the creatures of the sea.' And soon she fell pregnant. After nine months she gave birth to a baby boy, a beautiful one. But she did not remember her vow until her son reached the age of twenty-one. Then she remembered it one day, just like that.

She called her son, now a handsome young man. 'Here, you are to take this honey and oil to the sea creatures, for I made a vow a long time ago to give them this in return for you. I have just remembered my promise. It is good that you take it to them.'

The son obeyed, and taking the honey and oil he started walking towards the sea. He had walked halfway when he bumped into an old woman. 'What is it, Prince?' the old woman asked, 'Where are you off to and what are these that you are taking?' The Prince explained. 'I'll tell you what,' the old woman said, 'if you give them to me, I'll give you advice in exchange.' The Prince gave both the honey and the oil to her. 'Now, listen carefully, Prince,' she started, 'if you turn to the right and walk on for a little way you will come to a beautiful garden. Enter the garden and walk on regardless of what you might hear. There you will come to a pomegranate tree, pick some pomegranates and walk back. The pomegranates will open and from inside a beautiful girl will appear. She will ask for bread and water. If you give them to her she will live.' Then suddenly the old woman disappeared just as suddenly as she had appeared.

The Prince turned and walked the way he had been shown. After a while he came to a garden. He entered, it was a beautiful garden. He heard voices as he walked on. 'Turn back, this is not the place for you.' But he took no notice as he had been advised and continued walking. Eventually he came to a pomegranate tree, he picked some of the fruit and turned back. As he walked on one of the pomegranates opened and out of it a beautiful girl appeared. She asked for bread and water. He did not have any and she died. He walked on and a little while later another pomegranate opened and another beautiful girl appeared. Again, he did not have water and bread, so she died too.

In this way he lost all the pomegranates and girls except for one. By the time he got to the last one he had reached a spring and when the last pomegranate opened a beautiful girl came out. She was naked and wearing a beautiful necklace of beads. She asked for bread and water, so he gave her water from the spring but bread he did not have. 'If you wait here for me,' he said, 'I will go and get you bread. But first, I will help you to climb this orange tree, you can sit and wait for me there, and I will return soon with bread.' So the Pomegranate girl sat on top of the orange tree waiting for the Prince to return with some bread.

As she was sitting there, a red-faced maid came to the spring to fetch water. She saw the Pomegranate girl's reflection in the water and thought that it was her own reflection. 'How beautiful I am,' she cried. 'I don't have to work when I have such beauty.' She smashed the pot that she had in her hand and left. A little bit later she brought a child she had with her to bathe in the spring, she saw the reflection once more. 'But I am beautiful,' she cried again, and was about to throw the child on the rocks. The Pomegranate girl spoke and pleaded with her for the child's life. While they were talking, the child slipped away to safety. 'Who are you, what are you doing there?' the maid asked. She told the story, how she was waiting for the Prince. 'I love that necklace that you are wearing, can I just touch it please? Come down and I will just touch it.' The Pomegranate girl reluctantly climbed down from the orange tree, and the maid, pretending to touch it, opened it and took it off, then threw the Pomegranate girl into the spring and drowned her. She put the necklace on herself, climbed up the orange tree and sat waiting.

Presently, the Prince arrived with bread. 'You have been a long time, Prince,' she called out. The Prince could not believe his eyes when he saw her. 'Why has your face turned red?' he asked in astonishment. 'Why? Because of the sun, I have been sitting here for a long time waiting for you.' 'Why is your hair so ragged and dirty?' the Prince asked. 'Because it got caught in the branches of the tree,' she replied. 'And your legs are so scratchy and bruised,' said the Prince. 'That is because I have been climbing up and down the tree looking for you.' 'And where did you get that dress?' asked the Prince. 'I borrowed it from a maid.'

The Prince noticed that a beautiful *Nastaran* (sweet-briar) bush had grown beside the spring whilst he had been away. He loved it and picked some of its flowers, playing with the petals and stroking them as they walked. The maid took the flowers from him, broke them into pieces and scattered them. Then the Prince noticed a beautiful hat by the roadside. He picked it up and toyed with it as they walked. She snatched the hat from him and threw it away. Then the Prince saw a beautiful pigeon, and picked it up in his hand. He took it back with them to the palace and kept it as a pet, becoming very fond of it.

In time the maid fell pregnant and one day said, 'I have a craving for a dish of pigeon.' 'I will get you lots of pigeons then,' the Prince said. 'No, it is this particular pigeon of yours I want to eat,' she said. And so it was that the pigeon was killed and cooked for her. Where the pigeon's blood had spilled a tree grew, a *chenar* tree, a beautiful one. 'I want this tree to be cut down,' she said one day, 'to be made into a cradle for our baby,' and so it was done. There were some pieces of the tree left on the ground after it had been cut down, and an old lady who worked in the palace took one home with her. On returning to her house the next day, suddenly a beautiful young woman sprang from the fragment of wood, a daughter for her.

An announcement went round the town shortly after this that some of the King's horses were in a bad way and needed to be cared for, and that anyone who did a good job of this would get a reward. The girl asked the old woman to take one in, which she did. The horse was thin and sickly, near to death. The girl dipped her hair with water and brushed the garden with it. Beautiful, lush green grass grew all over the garden for the horse to eat. She cared for the horse lovingly and soon he grew healthy and strong. When it was returned to the King he granted her the highest reward.

One day another announcement went round the town that the necklace of the King's daughter-in-law had been broken and no one could thread it. Anyone who managed to do this would be richly rewarded. The Pomegranate girl volunteered to do this. 'I will do this, on one condition,' she announced when they were all seated waiting. 'That no one

should leave the room until I have finished threading it all.'
The room was full of people, including the Prince and his
wife. Then she sat down comfortably and started to thread
the beads as she sang, 'Once upon a time I was a
pomegranate on top of a tree, my beads, my beads. The
King's son came and picked me, brought me and put me on
top of an orange tree, my beads, my beads. A maid came
and took my beads, my beads, my beads. She threw me into
the water and I grew into a *Nastaran* bush, my beads, my
beads. The Prince picked me and cherished me, my beads,
my beads. The maid noticed, grabbed me, destroyed me and
scattered me, my beads, my beads. Then I turned into a
beautiful hat, my beads, my beads. The Prince found me
and caressed me lovingly, my beads, my beads. She
snatched me and threw me away, my beads, my beads.
Then I turned into a pigeon, my beads, my beads. When she
became pregnant, she craved a pigeon, my beads, my beads.
I was killed and fed to her, my beads, my beads. But I grew
into a pine tree where the blood was spilled, my beads, my
beads. I was cut down to be a cradle for her baby, my beads,
my beads. The old woman took a piece home, my beads, my
beads. Then I turned into a daughter for her, my beads, my
beads. One day my mother brought home a thin and dying
horse from the King to care for, my beads, my beads. It was
well looked after and soon grew healthy and strong, my
beads, my beads. Then, as it happened, the maid's necklace
broke, my beads, my beads.'
At this point the Prince's wife got up complaining of a
pain in her stomach, asking for the door to be opened that
she might go out, but the Prince reminded her that no one
should leave the room until all the beads were threaded and
she must keep to the rule.
'No one has managed to thread them, my beads, my
beads. So I came along on condition that no one should
leave the room before I had finished, my beads, my beads.'
With each utterance of the words, 'my beads, my beads',
a few of the beads were threaded. Now it was finished. The

Pomegranate girl threw the necklace towards the Prince's wife saying, 'Take it, what service it has done to its true owner, so may it do to you.' Now that the Prince realised that this was the true Promegranate girl, he kissed her on the forehead in quiet admiration of her wisdom and fortitude. And as for the maid? Some say she escaped on one of the Prince's horses, but whatever the truth, she was never seen again. All over the land, celebrations began which lasted seven days and seven nights, for the wedding of the Prince and the Pomegranate girl.

Aunt Zolikha's story was warmly received by Mahi's friends and family, renowned as she was for her retelling of traditional tales and folklore. At the evening progressed delicacies were brought around to eat – watermelon, pomegranates, quince, dried fruit, figs, dates, raisins, nuts and seeds, and sweets. Older children listened attentively, while the younger ones gradually fell asleep and were later carried home. That particular sitting lasted until the small hours of the following morning.

It was to become a very special one for Mahi because soon after the great uncle passed away. He was nearly a hundred and that was his last storytelling night, the last sitting he had held. Mahi felt proud to have held it in her house.

Mahi's Visit to Roghiieh

After the birth of Monir, Mahi had two more children, one boy and one girl. Now she considered her family to be complete. She was not going to have any more children, she decided. She was very happy with them, but she had to work very hard to look after them, to support them. Reza would leave her for months at a time to travel, looking for business, he would say. Sometimes he would take goods, bartering in other villages. He would take tea to one village, exchanging it for cotton wool in other villages. But quite often he would come home empty-handed. He had not made any profit. And sometimes he would return have made a loss.

'Give it up Reza,' friends and family would remark, 'this is no good, you are too soft to do business. You give way too easily.'

'Enough is enough. You never listen to me,' Mahi would complain bitterly. 'This is why I have to work doubly hard for the landlord, to scrape a living for the family. If only you had more sense.'

Mahi got the children to help her in any way she could, as indeed children helped in every household from about the age of four. She made a special effort to involve her daughter, Monir, who had been left blind with smallpox. 'Fetch a spoon for me,' she would say to her, or 'Get me some salt from the salt pot.' When she was about four, Mahi taught her how to spin wool with a little spindle. She would give her a chunk of wool to hold in her hand, then would show her how to stretch a piece, to thin it out, twist it around with the spindle, stretching it again as it twisted, then wrap it around the bottom and start again.

She would give corn to her daughter to go and feed the hens and would show her how to do it. Mahi would get her to hold the goats' heads in the evenings for her while she milked them, and would ask her to take away their babies, after a quick feed, and put them in their little sheds. Mahi would give animal skins to her children and their playmates to sit on and pull around. This was so that the skin could be cured, treated, stretched, worked on. So four or five children would sit on the skin and two or three children would pull it along, taking turns. It was great fun for them too, of course.

She often asked Monir to help her wind and unwind wool. For unwinding, she would get her to stretch her arms in front of her – showing her how far apart they should be – then put the loop of wool round her arms holding it tight, stiff. Then she would unwind it, turning it into a ball. And when she wanted to make it into a loop, it would be the same process, only in reverse. This looping and unlooping was necessary, so that the wool could be washed, dyed and then made into a ball again, to be used in making carpets and rugs, *kelims*.

Mahi showed her daughter how to make fire for the samovar. For this she would take a fire turner, which was a tiny little basket, made out of wire. Filling it with charcoal, she would sprinkle it with a bit of paraffin and set it alight. It had a long wire handle attached to it, a couple of metres in length. She would lift it up over her shoulder, circling it quickly in the air. The coals inside would burn more fiercely, then she would bring it down and put the fire into the samovar with fire tongs. Then she would put the metal lid on, and when the water boiled she would make the tea. She taught Monir to knit, encouraged her to cook. The older boy, Ali, helped gather wood for the fire, taking the sheep to run through the village square every morning and evening, from where the shepherd would take them to the hill for the day. She would get the children to help with cracking the wheat, churning butter and looking after the baby.

In the village everyone looked after the children, especially the babies. When they cried, anyone who happened to be nearby rushed to them, picked them up, played with them, talked to them, walked them around and swung them to sleep. But regular family life was rarely uninterrupted for long. Early one autumn morning, Reza woke up for morning prayer and found Mahi fully dressed and packing. 'Oh you are up, thank God, I have been waiting for you,' Mahi said, agitated.

'What is it?' Reza asked looking at his wife with concern, 'What is happening?'

'I had a dream, a horrible one, my mother was calling for me, I couldn't see her, but I could hear her, faint and feverish, she was calling for me. There is something wrong, she must be ill or something. I have to visit her, I have to go today. You must take me this morning.' She spoke fast but kept her voice low so as not to wake the children, as she handled the piles of clothes and nappies in front of her. 'The older children can stay with Aunt Zolikha, I am going to see her as soon as it is daylight. I'll take the baby with me of course.'

Reza kept looking at her in a daze, he watched her swift movements, listened to her clear words, her strong will fascinated him. He just sat there watching her as she organised the stuff she was taking. She had three different piles in front of her, her clothes, the baby's clothes and nappies. She had spread a large square cloth on the floor, put her pile of clothes in the centre, with the baby's clothes on top, then folded one corner of the cloth over pushing the edges underneath the pile. She then put the nappies on top of it, folding the opposite corner right round and securing it with a safety pin, then she put the two end corners together and tied them, making it into a bundle. It was ready to go in the sack. Now she had to think of something to take with them for lunch for the journey. It would take the whole day on a donkey ride to get to Khorbendeh, her mother's village.

Reza was still sitting there watching her, 'Aren't you going to your prayer?' she asked, looking at him straight, speaking in an urgent voice.

'Yes, yes. What about you?'

'I've done mine.' She got up to see to the picnic lunch. She put a few eggs on to boil, made a sandwich with cheese and some herbs, and she put some strained yoghurt in a bowl to take to her mother. She did not have much to take for her, this would do. To drink, she filled a bag made out of animal skin with water, then she put a few handfuls of raisins and mixed nuts in a cloth bag, wrapped them all in a small square heavy cloth, made it into a bundle, then put the whole lot into a sack.

Now it was time to attend to the animals. First she let out the hens and fed them, then she let out the goats and milked them in the yard and led them to the village square where the shepherd would take them with the others out to the fields, then she attended to the milk. It was her turn to take in the milk this week. She had eight goats in her care, they all belonged to the landlord and for better productivity she had an arrangement with five other women to take turns in collecting the milk. Each household would take the milk for a week. Every morning and evening after milking the goats, the women would take the milk to one house, where they would measure the milk with a bowl, so that they could remember how many bowls they had delivered each in that week.

When the women came with their buckets the first thing

Mahi told them was about her dream and that today she was going to visit her mother in Khorbendeh. They all listened to her with interest and sympathy. They rearranged the milk collection so that Khoshghadam would take over from that day. They discussed other things that had to be taken care of. Mahi normally enjoyed these gatherings, but today she was preoccupied with thoughts of her mother. The other women chatted, laughed, giggled and teased each other as they poured their milk into the large bucket measuring it with a medium-size heavy copper bowl.

'Six and a half, mine.'

'Mine has come to seven this morning.'

'Just over seven, call it seven,' the other woman announced with a giggle. Khoshghadam said she would look after the hens and the goats.

Mahi went to ask Aunt Zolikha to give her a hand, and she was back again before the children woke up. Everything had been arranged. Aunt Zolikha would look after Ali and the other two children, and would see that everything was all right in the house for Reza. She would give a hand with looking after the goats. There was nothing for her to worry about. She had complete trust in the women around her. They would take care of her house and the family just as they would their own.

She didn't feel like baking bread today, she would borrow a couple of loaves from Aunt Zolikha for their breakfast. Next time Mahi baked she would return the favour, that was fine.

The children were up now, she changed the baby, soaked the nappies. Khoshghadam was going to wash them later. She made the breakfast. She made the tea. She prepared a little hot milk for the other children, pouring it into a small bowl, and put in some pieces of bread. He took great pleasure in eating it, as he did every morning. He had to be as well fed as possible being a growing boy. If they did not manage to feed themselves they had at least to feed him as well as they could, he had to grow strong, he would look after them in their old age. Then she poured tea in a small glass for Reza, stirred in a few good lumps of sugar, and put it in front of him with some bread so that Reza could dip bread in this sweet tea and eat it. She did not sweeten her own tea, just put a small lump of sugar in her mouth and sipped the tea through it, then she had some bread, breastfeeding the baby at the same time. From the bit of bread left over she made a sandwich, spread with some strained yoghurt and some chopped onion and added it to the lunch for their journey.

She explained to the three older children what was happening, that she was going to Khorbendeh to see their grandma because she had had a dream and she was worried, and that they should stay with Aunt Zolikha and daddy would be back the next day. She would stay for a few days with the baby then they could come with daddy to pick her up. That was fine with them, they were always happy to stay with Aunt Zolikha, she always made a fuss of them. They were going to drop them off on the way but they all wanted to run over themselves straight away, which they did.

Reza got the donkey ready, fed, watered, groomed. Reza had a special affection for this one. He talked to him, patted him, as he got him ready for the journey. He regarded him as very special since a particular experience on the last journey when he had taken Ali with him. On the way back they had been travelling in the dark. When passing through a rocky, hilly area Ali had fallen off and the donkey nearly stepped on him, but when he had put his foot on him he realised it was the child and he took it off and just stood there. Wonderful animal. Reza told everyone of this experience.

When they set off the sun was just coming up. When they arrived in Khorbendeh the sun was just setting. Mahi had been right, Roghiieh had been very ill with pneumonia. 'I was thinking of sending you a message to come,'

Roghiieh said as mother and daughter embraced.

'I knew something was wrong, I dreamt it last night,' Mahi managed to say with her voice broken through tears, hugging her mother's feverish body.

'I already feel better now that you've come,' she said with a new strength in her voice. Reza stayed that night and left the next day. Mahi told him she would send a message when she was ready to return, or alternatively her brother could bring her home. If any of the children missed her too much, Reza could bring them to her.

Mahi took charge of the running of the house and looking after her mother from that day. Khadijeh, her sister, had done her best but she had also not been well for a long time and so was relieved at Mahi's arrival. Mahi's youngest brother, Hasan, was only eight years old, too young to be of any real help to their mother, and her middle brother, Ezatollah, was in Teheran. Too far away to return at short notice.

That first morning Mahi was up early to see Reza off, and then she began her morning prayers. Mahi performed ablution three times a day. At the end of each one she would have a quiet time with God, a kind of meditation. At times she would engage in a kind of communion with God, pouring out her heart and revealing her innermost secrets. She would admit to her shortcomings and make her requests. That morning she prayed devoutly for her mother's recovery, 'Oh Lord, give me strength, give my mother good health, to continue living her life honourably. She is a good woman, Oh Lord let her live.' She aired all her concerns, and worries, and asked for help in her distress. 'Give me vision,' she said, 'in this difficult time, give me wisdom, help me do my best for my mother and my family, and for their future wellbeing.' In this communion she also said a prayer for the dead, a blessing for the spirits, 'May their spirits be at rest.' Mahi believed the spirits of dead loved ones looked over her family, protected them and shared their concerns. And now she called on their help with all her heart.

For the remainder of that day, and during the many days that followed, Mahi devoted herself to helping her mother get better. In nursing Roghiieh Mahi used herbs and massage. A kind of massage called 'stepping massage' was particularly helpful. For this, Roghiieh laid on her tummy on the floor and Mahi, who was said to be lightfooted, stepped on and off her back with one foot, placing it lengthways, gently massaging as she went. She started on one side, and did this from top to bottom, until both her sides had been treated a few times. She would step on the middle part of her mother's back with both feet, standing across the spine and gently walking up and down. From time to time Mahi heard crackling noises which were a good sign of the stiffness easing. At first Mahi gave Roghiieh a general massage all over using essential oils. Then Roghiieh was given plenty of water melon juice to drink. She also had to take certain oils orally and inhale others. Many different herbs were used as part of the treatment. Some were soaked overnight, and she would take them the next day, some were boiled or brewed, some steamed.

When Roghiieh's backache was severe Mahi used cup massage on her, a special treatment needing expert knowledge and experience. Mahi was especially good at this, and was often called upon in the neighbourhood to give it to people. For this she would take a cup and apply pressure with it to the painful part of the back. She used her hands for a lighter type of massage for less severe problems.

After being massaged Roghiieh was given hot food and herbal drinks, then would sleep, covered up to bring on a sweat. Every effort was made to let her sleep as long as possible, to aid her recovery. Roghiieh was not woken up, but left to wake of her own free will. Mahi chose particular foods that were easy for her mother to digest.

70

She often cooked a baby chicken, simmering it gently, before adding rice or noodles and some parsley, serving it with a little lemon juice. She also cooked rice flour in milk with ground almonds, rice pudding, clear soups, and tender lamb.

Mahi and Roghiieh made a vow to visit the shrine together next spring, when her recovery was complete. Meanwhile people visited her throughout the day, to keep her company, and to wish her a speedy return to good health. Everyone in the village felt it their duty to pop in to see Roghiieh. But the illness was severe and Roghiieh's recovery was slow.

The Great Uncle's Death

Mahi's stay in Khorbendeh was coming to an end. She had been there for two months looking after Roghiieh, who had almost recovered from this very bad attack of pneumonia. She had been very ill but she had pulled through.

'Thanks to you, Mahi,' she had said many times. 'Had it not been for you being here and looking after me so well, I don't think I would have survived.'

'No, mother, it is not me, it is the strength within you that pulled you through.'

A message had been sent to Reza to come and collect Mahi, and he was sure to come any day now.

'Maybe tomorrow,' she said one night.

That night, Mahi's great uncle who lived with Roghiieh returned from a journey. He had been away for a while visiting his grand-daughter and her family who lived in a distant village. He often travelled. He would take off into the forest with his donkey and would be away for days. He liked solitude he said, spending time with the creatures of the forest.

'What is there in the forest, uncle?' the youngsters would ask, each vying for his attention.

'There is a wealth of knowledge and experience there. You just have to open yourself to it,' he would reply.

'Can we see it and experience it if we come with you, great uncle?'

'You'll know when you can see it, then you can visit.'

'Do you learn all your stories from the creatures in the forest, great uncle?' the young ones asked.

He always laughed, replying, 'Yes, they teach me wonderful stories. We all tell each other stories in the forest, the trees, plants and creatures. We tell each other great secrets.'

Great uncle's stories were special and the way he told them made them even more special. He was often invited to other villages and people would travel long distances to hear him, arriving on donkeys for an evening of story-telling.

He was nearly a hundred years old. He had survived his wife. Two of his son had died in the Kurdish liberation struggle. Since his wife's death he had moved in to live with Roghiieh. It was believed that he had healing powers. He would lay hands on the sick and they were convinced that it made them better. He had been seen many times in the war zone attending to the wounded fighters and they were often the ones who recovered, it was said.

'You have been seen there, uncle,' young men just back from fighting would say.

'But he has been here with us,' the family would protest.

'I have been in both places.'

'At one time?'

'At one time.' He would not explain more than that.

The night of his return he did not want any dinner, he said.

'But why?' Roghiieh asked. 'You can't go to bed without any dinner, you must have something.'

He had arrived after they had finished dinner.

'Please let me bring you some food,' Mahi said, 'just a little, you must have something.'

'No, I don't feel like anything, not tonight. Tonight it is better for me not to have anything at all,' he had said, with a mysterious look on his face.

'Are you feeling all right, uncle?' Roghiieh asked, looking at him intently.

'Oh yes, I'm alright. I just don't feel like eating tonight. I am going, Roghiieh. I have been waiting for you to get well. It is time for me to go now.'

'Go where, uncle?' Roghiieh and Mahi both uttered in surprise together.

'Go to the other world, you know. I have had enough of this world, I am ready to go.'

'Don't talk like that, uncle. God forbid. Nothing is the matter with you, is there?'

'Nothing has to be the matter, it is just time for me to go, and that time is tonight, I feel,' he explained coolly and calmly. 'I know when I am dying.'

Mahi was looking at him in dismay. 'Maybe you have a cold, uncle?'

'No, no cold, not this time. God bless you, Mahi, you looked after your mother very well, you have brought her back to life, you are a good girl. May God keep you and bless you for your children.' He kissed Mahi on the forehead.

They had some tea together and some fruit then uncle, after saying his evening prayer, got prepared for bed. Then he wished everyone good night and with a long look left for his room.

Early in the morning when Roghiieh got up to say her morning prayer before sunrise, there was no sign of uncle. Usually he would be the first to get up for prayer. Soon Mahi was up as well to say her prayer. When she had finished, Roghiieh said, 'There is no sign of uncle. This is unlike him.'

'I will go and wake him for prayer,' Mahi said. After a few moments she was back. 'I have bad news, mother,' she announced, 'great uncle is dead.' He had died in his sleep. Mahi rushed next door and told Habib. When Sakineh, his wife, joined them Mahi, Roghiieh and Khadije were crying aloud in the room, sitting around the body, hitting themselves, especially Roghiieh who was tearing at her hair. The four women cried together for a long while. A couple of neighbours who had been told the news came and joined them. Roghiieh fainted. Masoomeh from next door boiled the samovar to make tea, she dropped an egg into the samovar for a minute, then cut the top off, stirred it, and gave it to Roghiieh to drink. 'Come on, you have to drink it, it will do you good.' While Mahi and Sakineh sponged Roghiieh's face with cold water and held burning daub under her nose to bring her round, tea was passed around to everyone, and an especially strong cup to Roghiieh with lots of sugar, which they persuaded her to drink. They massaged her back, and got her to lie down and keep calm. Masoomeh saw that the children had some breakfast and tried to get the others to eat something but they wouldn't. Presently the men arrived to take the body away to the mosque. There they heated water and washed his body with soap and warm water. It was dried and measured for a shroud, three lengths of fine, white cotton were brought. The first layer was called *shah kafan*, the Great Shroud. He was wrapped in it from head to toe, very carefully. Every part of his body was wrapped in the cloth, his toes, his fingers, and the back of his neck, every bit of him was covered. Then he was wrapped in a second layer from head to toe, and the last layer he was wrapped in was called *shroud kafan*, which was tied both ends with a strip of the same cloth. Then the body was wrapped in a large blanket of pure wool, black and white, hand-knitted, and rather beautiful. This was the blanket that the bedding in the house was usually wrapped in and made into a large cushion which lay against the wall for people to lean against when they sat down. Then it was put into a *Taboot*, a large container made out of wood on which the body was carried to the cemetery. A large scarf covered the *Taboot*, it was made out of *terme*, a beautiful multi-coloured scarf with tassels of the most expensive material. Then the priest came and read verses from the Koran.

All this was done by the menfolk, whilst at home Mahi got down to clearing up, preparing and organising, but she had to keep a special eye on Roghiieh so that she would not exert herself too much, not distress herself. 'This will only set your recovery back, Mother,' she kept reminding her, 'try to keep calm.' She got her young brother, Hasan, to run errands. They had to find a way of letting Mahi's brother Ezat know, but that would have to be done later.

Mahi sent Hasan to get tea, sugar and dates. She arranged for messages to be sent to other villages to notify relatives and friends. There was still much to be done in preparation for the funeral. Khadijeh was overcome with distress, Sakineh was too lazy to help, so everything was left to Mahi. The neighbours were more help, especially Masoomeh who kept offering people drinks, looking after the children and the animals.

Everybody went to change their clothes. They all wore black. Mahi did not have any black clothes there so she borrowed from Masoomeh.

Then they put down a mattress with an eiderdown on top of it covered with a beautiful handwoven coverlet, a *sajaddeh*, similar in texture to a *kelim*, but superior in quality. On top of that they spread out his clothing. They sat round it crying, hitting themselves, tearing at their hair, some were even scratching their faces. People were coming in and out constantly, offering their condolences and saying their prayers for him. Both at home and at *Masjed*, the mosque entrance, a youngster stood at the door holding a jar of rosewater, spraying the water on people's hands as they came in.

Meanwhile, Habib together with Mamad-Ali and other cousins had gone to dig and prepare the grave. It was late morning when they started to carry the body to the cemetery. They took the *taboot*, coffin, on their shoulders and began the journey to the grave. People came and took their turn in carrying the *taboot*, throughout the journey, relatives and close friends especially wanted to take part in carrying it. When they arrived the grave was ready. An area two metres by three metres had been dug up, about half a metre in depth. Then within that another hole had been dug, now lined with stone and big enough for a body to lie in. The old man's body was laid on it, on his side facing south, the direction of Mecca. Then it was covered over with large flat stones, making sure every bit was covered. Earth was poured in to fill the hole and the earth stamped down to make it firm. Two large stones were put on the grave. Finally, one large flat stone was put on vertically, sunk in at one end on the right hand side to show that this body was male. Verses from the Koran were recited over his grave. 'Oh Lord, I thank thee and worship thee only. Oh Lord, guide me and show me the right way, as you have shown all Muslims, but not those who have been the subject of your anger. God is one, has not been born, nor given birth. Only you I admire and worship. I come from you and I am returning back to you.'

The women prepared a large bowl of mud at home and smeared some on the head and shoulders of close relatives as they entered the house, from the young to the elderly. On the third day it was the turn of the women to visit the cemetery. A large group of them arrived in the morning, greeting the dead, one by one, as they passed the graves. When they reached the great uncle's grave they flung themselves over it, wailing and howling, hitting themselves on their heads, tearing their hair, scratching their faces, and pouring soil over their heads, believing that in this way their love and attachment for great uncle would return back to the earth. When they had exhausted themselves they recited prayers and verses from the Koran before leaving.

That day Sakineh helped Mahi cook a large quantity of halva, which would be served in the mosque and in the neighbourhood. It was called *Sham-Ghariban*, the Dinner for the Strangers, the dead person being the stranger. The family believed that the uncle's spirit would come back to the house to check everything over, and if they were happy so it would be happy and would expect food to be provided and prayers to be said for him.

Mahi was cutting up the halva in a large tray to be carried to the mosque when Reza arrived, he had come to take her back. He was a great support for Mahi. He stayed for three days then left on his own to return again for the fortieth-day ceremony. Mahi and Roghiieh made sure a light was kept on in the house, if the family were not in, for great uncle's spirit. It was said that his spirit appeared at times to the loved ones, especially the children.

One day during the first week after great uncle's death, his great grandson was sitting in great uncle's room with his mother and grandmother. The boy was only a year old, but had been very fond of the old man, and they had often played together. All of a sudden, he started waving his arms frantically with great excitement and joy, shouting 'Uncle! Uncle!' and pointing up to someone as if saying 'pick me up'.

'Look at him, why is he doing this?' said his mother with astonishment.

'It is all right, leave him,' the grandmother replied. 'He is seeing his great-grandfather's spirit.'

On the eve of the seventh day they all went to the cemetery again for a big gathering. They distributed food and dates and a special sort of halva, made only for such occasions, and again on the eve of his fortieth day, but because he had three children, three days were taken off so that the thirty-seventh day after his death was referred to as the fortieth day. Every Friday evening from that time onwards the family visited the grave, distributing dates and halva.

Reza arrived the day before the fortieth ceremony. He had brought Ali with him, and helped with the preparations which Mahi was glad of. When the day was over, he asked Mahi gently, 'Do you think you can come home now, is your mother well enough to be left?' She did not reply straight away.

That night when they having dinner at Habib's, Sakineh asked, 'When are you leaving, Mahi?' Mahi hesitated to answer.

Roghiieh said, 'I'm perfectly all right, Mahi, you can go now.'

'Are you sure?' Mahi said.

'I'm absolutely sure, you should go back, take charge of your own life. I am all right, I'll manage.'

When they returned from Habib's house, Mahi started packing. They had to leave in the early morning otherwise the heat would be too much for the children. It had been a long stay for Mahi, and she was glad to be returning home at last.

Khadijeh's Visit to Teheran

Mahi's family had gradually moved to Teheran in search of a better life. Her father had been a gambler from a very young age and had gone to Teheran many years earlier looking for excitement, taking his eight-year-old middle son, Ezatollah, with him. Soon after he had died as a result of drugs and dissolution, leaving his son all alone to fend for himself.

Ezatollah had taken refuge in a motorway cafe where he had washed the dishes and run errands for his keep. He gradually worked his way up, washing dishes, cleaning, then serving, and all the while teaching himself to read and write, asking for help in this respect from the customers and anyone literate he could find coming in and out of the cafe. He showed enormous perseverance, worked very hard, and because he was particularly good at maths he was eventually asked to look after the accounts. Then he became assistant manager and finally took over the running of the cafe, becoming a shareholder in it.

He started sending his earnings back to his family in the village and as soon as he had a reasonable income he had brought his mother, his youngest brother, Hasan and his niece, Khoshsahat to Teheran. A little later he brought his uncle and his family, also helping them to make a living in the city. And now Mahi was living in Teheran with her brother too. She often remembered how she had persuaded Reza to leave the village and go to the capital, where her family were, and where they could escape the landlord's cruelty. They had heard so many good things about the city. But many other peasants were pouring into Teheran looking for work and, once there, Reza could only find occasional jobs, labouring or cleaning out pools in people's gardens. Mahi was able to find a steady stream of work, as a washerwoman. It was hard work, particularly in winter, but at least she earned a little money to buy food for the family. The fact that Reza did not have a steady job put a lot of strain on their already weak relationship and eventually Mahi left him after one particularly severe argument, moving to her brother's house. Her husband's subsequent death which came suddenly, soon after her move, was a shock to the whole family.

Mahi's sister, Khadijeh had not moved to Teheran. When Roghiieh and the other members of her family left Khorbendeh it was decided she would join them later. She stayed with Habib, her older brother who had his own family. 'She should be here and help in the house,' Habib had said. Khadijeh dreaded the thought of living with Habib, he was a ruthless man and the hardships he subjected his family to, especially the females, were public knowledge, people talked about it.

Sakineh, Habib's wife, was a large and lazy woman, she was pregnant every year for thirty years, so Khadijeh had to do all her housework for her during the day and in the nights she worked on carpets. Habib beat up Khadijeh frequently, saying she wasn't quick enough in her work. She worked very hard, day and night, and ate very little but drank plenty of water. 'This sister of mine lives on water alone,' Habib said, mockingly. 'Just as well, otherwise she will get too fat.' She wept a lot. 'She has to weep to get rid of all that water she takes in,' he added cruelly. He always found something with which to mock her and to laugh at her. Khadijeh cried often, she cried noisily and heartily and felt better afterwards. A good cry, that was what she needed, that was what energised her and enabled her to carry on her work relentlessly.

So she lived with Habib for many years, until one day she announced, 'I want to live separately, I want to have my own home.' This had outraged Habib and Sakineh.

'You are mad, this is another sign of your madness,' Habib had said. At first they didn't take it too seriously but, when she insisted, she had been severely told off. 'You have to stay put, it is impossible for you live alone, out of the question, you must stop thinking of it at once.' It was unheard of, no woman lived on her own anywhere, not here nor anywhere else, it was unwise, unsafe, a young, sick, divorced woman living on her own, what will people say, it will give the family a bad name, she will be ostracised and so will the family.

'Who will do the work here anyway, if you leave,' Sakineh had said.

'But I will come and do your work, I won't leave you in difficulty, I just want to have my own place to sleep in the night, that's all, just a place of my own.'

'Who will help me with the carpet in the night?' There was always a carpet in Habib's house either belonging to the landlord or sometimes Habib would provide the material and then sell a carpet without giving any of the money to Khadijeh. 'Just keeping you is a big burden on us,' he had said many times. She could feel now that her eyesight was getting strained with all those long nights working on a carpet in the poor lighting of an oil lamp, which Habib insisted should be turned down to save paraffin.

Now that she had made up her mind to move away to live alone, nothing was going to stop her, not even Habib's savage beatings, Sakineh's scorn, and the disapproval of family and neighbours. No amount of persuasion or advice from the elders of the village would change her mind. 'It is my life, after all. What do you think will happen to me living alone? Just because no women live on their own doesn't mean that it cannot be done. What shame will I bring my family? I have brought all the shame already, with my divorce, and the illness that followed, nothing can be worse than those. I have done the worse damage to myself and my family, I can't help it. With this I will be less of a burden on you all, you don't have to feel responsible for me, I can run my own life, I just want to be left alone, that's all.' No amount of advice, pressure, persuasion, insistence, threats or beatings worked.

A little house had become vacant not far from Habib's, the previous tenants had moved to Teheran in search of work. It had been empty for a while and she had had her eye on it. In the end they had to give in. She was starving herself to death. 'I don't want her blood on my hands,' Habib said, throwing her few possessions out of the house one day in fury after having given her a severe beating. He was exasperated by her constant crying and the deep depression she had sunk into. He could take it no longer. From that day on she took refuge in her lonely little house. She made it her home. She had never felt so tranquil as in this little home of hers. 'It is all mine, mine only, I can do whatever I like in it. I can laugh. I can cry. I can talk. I can dream freely. No one to watch over me or to nag me. I have never been so free and happy, I should have done this long ago.'

Khadijeh was shunned, avoided and scorned. Some pitied her, 'She is sick, she doesn't know what she is doing,' people said. Her family, whose advice she had rejected, stopped communicating with her. It was some years later that they started coming round, and invited her to come to see them in Teheran and to consider living there with them for good. So Khadijeh agreed to pay a visit to her family.

'I wouldn't want to live there, but I'm longing to see you all, so I'll just come for a visit and stay for a bit. I may not have long to live,' she had said. 'I want to see you all before I go.'

She had been saving up for this visit for some time. Normally any money she made from carpet-making Habib took from her. 'I am in debt, give me what you have and I will give it back to you.' When she handed it over that was the end of that, she never saw it again. Being in debt was the key word that softened her. 'He was in debt, he said he would give it back to me this time,' she would say innocently to friends. Whatever she earned periodically Habib forced it out of her. But now she had managed to save enough for her trip.

Khadijeh had been looking forward to and preparing for this journey for a long time, making presents of beautiful embroidery, patchwork, knitwork, she had to make something for everyone, children and babies included, for all members of the family and friends. The day arrived. It was a beautiful summer's day. Habib himself was to take her to Teheran. 'You must come back in the autumn, we need you here,' he said with authority. They set off early in the morning on a donkey, driving to Dameh, the nearest town, which would take half a day, from there they would take a coach. Khadijeh had not been on a coach or any vehicle before and she was excited by the adventure.

When they arrived in Teheran the sun was setting. The family had been waiting for them in the coach station, her mother, Mahi, her daughter Khoshsahat, her son-in-law and her youngest brother, Hasan. Khadijeh had her daughter brought up by Roghiieh ever since she was born. After the rest of the family had moved to Teheran, Khoshsahat had visited her mother in the village once in a while, and each time she had been heartbroken to see the conditions under which her mother lived, a broken woman in absolute destitution. They did not have much to talk about and Khadijeh cried constantly and said what a bad mother she had been, and each time Khoshsahat had come away with a deep sense of sadness about her mother, about how miserable and how lonely she was. She felt helpless, unable to do anything or change anything for her.

Khadijeh was pleased now, as her daughter had married at last and had her own home. She had been deprived of this experience, but she had come now to see her daughter in her own home, and to bless it. Khadijeh rushed towards her daughter, embraced her, showered her with kisses, two women crying together, hugging each other, tasting each other's tears. She held her, hugging her for a long while, crying, talking to her, 'Your mother ought to be sacrificed to you, what have I done for you.' She had a long cry, she cried noisily, heartily, she always cried in that manner. After a while she pulled away from Khoshsahat, who would not let her go. Then she embraced the others, still crying, kissing them. Mahi had just lost her husband, and the two sisters cried in each other's arms, mixing their tears. The family had to separate them. Then she hugged and kissed her younger brother, Hasan, and then gave a brief hug to her mother, Roghiieh, whom she regarded as responsible for her predicament, by forcing her into marriage so many years ago. Then she was introduced to Mahamad Hussein, her son-in-law, she put her arms round his neck and was just about to kiss him but they pulled her away all embarrassed. 'It's all right, I just wanted to kiss him, I can kiss him, can't I? He's like my son.' With the children she embraced them one by one, some she had not met, she hugged them, talked to them, weeping all the time, 'Your aunt should be sacrificed to you, I'm ashamed at the kind of aunt I have been to you, I have let you down, haven't I? I haven't done anything for you. I am ashamed of myself. I am not worthy of being an aunt to you, I haven't done the duties of an aunt, I have failed you as an aunt.'

Next day they were to receive many visitors – relatives, friends and neighbours came to see Khadijeh to welcome her. She was to meet many new members of her family on the side of her son-in-law. She was surrounded by people for many days, being invited to their houses. Khadijeh had a kind of childlike innocence to her, she was like a mirror reflecting everything inside her. This caused the family embarrassment at times, especially with people they didn't know every well. One day when she was staying with Mahi, an acquaintance came by for a cup of tea. The conversation had turned to Javad, the young bachelor next door, Mahi had told Khadijeh about Javad in confidence, that he had his eye on her and that he was divorced with a little boy who was staying with the mother. The story went round that his wife had divorced him because of his impotence. 'What do I want him for, if he can't even satisfy a woman?' Mahi had said jokingly. The acquaintance remarked in fun, 'I think Javad fancies you, Mahi. He needs a wife, doesn't he?'

It was Khadijeh who responded, 'Yes, but Mahi says, what does she want him for, if he is not even capable of satisfying a woman?' Then immediately her voice dropped, saying, 'Mahi, why did you poke me under the *korsi*, did you want me to stop what I was saying, what did you do that for, I wasn't lying, that's what you said, wasn't it?'

Mahi went red with embarrassment, 'But I didn't poke you sister,' she said with a shaking voice.

'Yes, you did, you gave me a poke under the *korsi* as if to say stop.'

'She is funny in the head,' they would explain to strangers.

One night the two sisters had a long heart-to-heart.

'Mahi, it is so wonderful to see you settled here happily in Teheran, managing so well on your own,' Khadijeh started.

'Yes sister,' Mahi replied. She always addressed her as 'sister' because Khadijeh was her senior. 'I am happy now, but it hasn't been easy, I assure you.'

'No, surely not,' Khadijeh agreed. 'How could it have been easy, uprooting yourself and coming to Teheran with four children, then losing first your husband, and then your baby daughter. Tell me how it happened – how you lost your little girl?'

'Oh, I hoped you wouldn't ask me that, sister.' Mahi sighed with great sadness. 'It makes my heart ache whenever I am reminded about her. I try to forget, but I never can. Yes, my baby died and I feel responsible.'

'Why?' Khadijeh asked.

'I lost my crowned lady. I had given her the name Khanomtaj, the crowned lady. That was what she was to me, my beautiful daughter. She withered away, starved to death.'

'But tell me how, Mahi,' Khadijeh insisted gently.

'Well, soon after we arrived in Teheran I had to look for work. Reza couldn't get a steady job, so I had to do something, anything which would bring in some money to feed us. After much searching, the only work I could find was to go to people's houses and do their washing. It was hard work but I didn't mind. I was prepared to do anything – anything which was honourable. My only problem was, what would happen to my baby? If only I could take her with me. 'I have a ten-month-old baby, do you mind if I bring her with me?' I suggested to my first lady. 'I can strap her to my back, so my work won't suffer, I won't let it, I promise.' 'Oh no, no,' she said indignantly, 'that won't do.' She nearly dismissed me simply for having suggested it, so I had to leave Khanomtaj behind. I had to choose between her and the welfare of the whole family.

'I had to go to work every day with the sunrise and did not get back till late afternoon, and then I had my own work to do, shopping, cooking, washing, fetching water for bathing, and cleaning, all had to be done at the end of each day. And, with six of us living in one small basement room, it wasn't easy. I had no time or energy left for poor Khanomtaj, let alone milk in my breasts. My milk dried up and she would desperately suck my empty breast, until it ached and I pulled away from her. I can still hear her whimper. She did not cry, she would just whimper for a minute or two, and then go quiet and lay there, poor soul, as though she knew it was dangerous to make demands.

She gradually withered away, my crowned lady. I can still almost feel the pain in her whimper, the ache in my breast, the cruelty with which I pulled it from her mouth. How could I?' Mahi burst out. 'And one day,' she continued, weeping, 'I came home from work to find her cold, dead body. I've been pleading with my God for mercy and forgiveness ever since. I feel responsible for her death, and I wonder if I will ever be forgiven.' Mahi cried noisily.

Khadijeh hugged her. 'Oh Mahi, my little sister, it wasn't your fault, it wasn't your doing. You did your very best. You had to choose between her and the whole family, as you said, and anyone would have done what you did.' Mahi wept in her sister's arms. Khadijeh continued, 'But you still have many good things in your life. You have three children and, what is more, you have your independence. You are young and capable, you should be happy – unlike me, I haven't got anaything to be happy about.'

'But you've got your daughter,' said Mahi, concerned.

'Not really,' Khadijeh murmured sadly, as the memories flooded back and she opened up the wounds of her past, going over with Mahi her forced marriage, her one night of married life, her husband's brutal treatment of her, her divorce, her breakdown, and the birth of her daughter.

Khadijeh had been a tall, slender girl, with long black shiny hair. She normally plaited her hair into six thick plaits reaching her lower back. When unplaited her hair reached her buttocks and she had to lift it out of the way when sitting down. She had been an outstanding beauty, with powerful eyes that saw right through you. Many young men had fallen for her and would have given anything to marry her.

It was Bahram, the son of the landlord, who had set eyes on her one summer evening, years ago, at the spring. 'I had gone to fetch drinking water from the spring on my own that evening. I was standing there watching the fish in the water, you know how I love watching them, they have always fascinated me. Such beauty and magic, their colours, shapes, movements have always filled me with wonder. It is their freedom that I always longed for, they are such graceful creatures. I was mesmerised. As you know we villagers never eat fish, not like you lot in Teheran, you eat fish, I don't know how you can do such a thing. Many things amaze me here and this is one of them, you people eating fish, we never touch them. We regard them with sanctity and reverence as you know, I hope you haven't forgotten that, Mahi. Anyway, I was telling you what happened that evening.

'I had met Morad in that spot, that very day, a year earlier. I had gone to fetch water. I was absorbed watching the fish. Mother used to say, "Come back soon, don't stay there until midnight with the fish." Morad had arrived to water his horse. He was on his way to our house, he said, to collect a parcel for Uncle Timor. He was off to the frontier, to the war, the next day. He was tall, strong, handsome, he held his head high as he spoke, his strong, clear voice is still in my ear, I can hear him still, he spoke with hope, "We will win, it is just a matter of time."

'We stood there for a long while watching the fish together, absorbed in them, fascinated, full of admiration. Then he spoke, "They are free." This was also in my thoughts, it was my preoccupation, the thing for which I longed. I looked at him, our eyes met, we merged. In a flash he had filled me, I was free, he had entered me, enriched me, freed me. I took him inside me, we floated together as one. It was sweet. It engulfed me, the sweetness, it seemed everlasting and it has remained with me all these years with the same strength, these were the best moments I have ever had in life.

'We talked together in the moonlight well into the night. We talked of freedom, that very thing that connected us together, the struggle for it, the war. He told me of the death and destruction of the Kurdish people at the hands of government troops. He told me of the history of the struggle. "I want to come with you," I said. "Take me with you." He took me in his arms and held me tight. "I want you to come," he murmured, burying his face in my hair, I felt his breathing on my neck, it warmed me through. "I can do a lot there, you know, a lot," I said, feeling strong with his agreement. "I can help with the wounded, I have been teaching myself all about treatment and nursing. I have collected many herbs and oils and medicines, I know a lot about them, how to use them and so on, this has been my dream, to go to the war zone. I can go in men's clothes if need be."

'He was listening to me, holding me tight. I was talking fast. "I will wear men's clothes. I will cut off my hair. I can even speak like a man. Shall I show you?" Shall I show you, I said in a deep voice. With this he burst out into loud laughter, we both did, we both laughed and laughed, rolling with each other. When parting he held me tight, looked in my eyes and said, "Will you promise me one thing, will you wait for me?" "I will come, I will come and join you," I replied. "You'll see." We held each other in silence for a long time.

'Now standing there watching the fish, I could see Morad, I could hear his voice, feel his breath, I heard the neighing of his horse, his face was in my mind, his voice in my ears, I was filled with desire for him. I felt jubilant, I felt like throwing myself in his arms, I turned, only to find that it wasn't him standing next to me, it was someone else. I had to rub my eyes, look again, no, it wasn't Morad. The man standing there had his eyes fixed on me, he looked as though he was going to swallow me any minute, he was a stranger, he was not one of us I could tell by his clothing. I was repelled. A kind of sudden disgust filled me, replaced all that jubilation and expectation. This disturbed me, distressed me, I felt angry, invaded by him, taking away my ecstasy like that. I looked him straight in the eyes, frowning, my anger must have come through, he was transfixed, speechless, just staring at me. Then I took up my pot and started to leave. "Whose daughter are you?" he asked with a stammer, to which I did not reply and walked off. "Where do you live?" he shouted after me. I ignored him and walked on fast. I headed straight on home with an empty pot.

'Three days later two strange women visited us, they had come for *Khastegari*, the 'asking process' whereby a bride was chosen. "You do not know what strange luck has come your way," one of them said to mother. "Your daughter is to be the bride of Bahram, the landlord's son." The one who had invaded my privacy that evening had been one of the landlord's sons. How many sons or daughters he had no one knew, legal or illegal. They all lived in Teheran or abroad, so the story went. Bahram, who was visiting from Teheran, had insisted on marrying me after that encounter by the spring. "She is not suitable for you, she is the daughter of a peasant, you can have her if you want, we will bring her to you for a night," he'd been told, "but not for marriage." But marriage he wanted it to be. He'd been ill for a few days with a high fever. "All right, do it," the father had ordered. "Let there be a wedding if he insists, he'll get rid of her soon enough." He had instructed his deputy to take the matter in hand and arrange a marriage.

'I was coming up to fifteen then and had refused many *Khastegaris*. I wanted to be free, I wanted to be a nurse, I wanted to go to the war zone, I was waiting for my chance. It was the freedom I was after and for that I wanted to go to the war zone, and yet they wanted to cage me. "If you force me into marriage," I told mother, "to this man or any other man, I'll kill myself just like my friend Hamideh did." I will run away, if I can't kill myself, I thought. I will cut off my hair, I will wear men's clothes. I was now able to talk with a man's voice, I used to take to the woods and practise speaking in a deep voice, just like a man. No one could tell it was a woman speaking in a man's voice, I was so good at it. There in the war zone, I would care for the soldiers, look after the wounded, treat them, soothe them, help them to recover their health. I could join them in the fight as well, I could learn quickly. I dreamt day and night of this.

'My friend Hamideh had hung herself three days after her wedding. On her wedding night she did not allow her husband to touch her. The next day as soon as he was out of the room she locked herself in. Three days later when they broke down the door she had hanged herself from the ceiling, still in her wedding dress. She'd put the chest in the middle of room, piled all the bedding on it, used the pinroll to hang her scarf through the skylight, put it round her neck and then had pushed off the bedding with her feet. Hamideh had fallen in love with Ghasem but was forcefully married off to Hidar who was the son of one of the managers to the landlord, a ruthless manager too, a real blood-sucker. A few days before the wedding she took to the woods with Ghasem, I arranged their meeting. They made love there. She told me all about it. He was to leave for the war the next day and a week later his body was brought to the village and buried next to hers. It was said that he was killed on the same day that Hamideh killed herself.

'Hamideh was my best friend, she and I spent a lot of time together, we made knitwear for the soldiers, socks, scarves, gloves, pullovers. The day I met Morad he had come to collect a scarf I had knitted for Uncle Timor. But Hamideh had knitted a spectacular one for Ghasem, people couldn't stop admiring it and everyone came to have a look at it before it was sent off. Everyone envied Hamideh in that village for her talent. The scarf had at its cente a heart, surrounded by flowers, greenery, a tree and branches. A single red rose grew out of the heart. The background was sky blue with reds, whites, browns, purples, yellows worked into it.

'When Ghasem's body was brought to the village to be buried, her scarf was wrapped tight around his body right down to his waist, the heart with the red rose on his chest.

'Meanwhile my own wedding preparations got under-way. Nothing I could do seemed to have any effect, they would not listen to me. "The boy has fallen in love with you, he has been severely ill, he will give you a good life. We can't say no to the landlord's wishes, if we did they will take you by force, you know that, we have no choice, it has to go ahead, this is your fate, what will be will be, so let us just make it honourable by agreeing to it. Everyone will benefit from it. This is an honour for the family to connect with the landlord," father had said, "and for the village that one of its daughters be chosen to marry the landlord's son."

'The ball started rolling, the wedding was arranged. Because father could not provide much of a dowry for me, the amount agreed to on Bahram's side was 1250 *rial*. This would be paid to me on divorce, if Bahram divorced me that is, but if I decided to divorce him I would not be entitled to it and neither could I take my dowry back. The injustice of it touched my bones.

'The date was set by Bahram's family. The engagement and the wedding were going to be on the same day. Mother checked out the suitability of the day they had suggested for the wedding with the wise man of our village. He did not agree with the date they had in mind, but they said they had consulted their own wise man and he assured them that it was suitable. Mother believed that they had lied to us, that they did not really believe in these things, they were modern, they were educated, they had been to Europe.

'Mother scraped together whatever she could for my dowry. Bahram's family wanted the wedding to be as soon as possible. The date was set for two weeks time. Five or six women were set to work on making the wedding dress. Our house was full all the time. The night before the wedding a big pot of henna was soaked and some young girls in the neighbourhood coloured the backs of their hands, their finger-nails and toe-nails. The music played and there was singing and dancing.

'The celebrations had started three days earlier in our

house. Next morning I was to be taken to the *hammam*, the public bath house, accompanied by a group of women, a few young girls of my age, a few older women and some younger women. There, they cleansed me and scrubbed me until I was raw, my pubic hair was removed for the first time, using a herbal mixture. I had seen women use this mixture many times before, it was soaked, applied and left for a while to take effect and then washed off, all the hair came away with it. This cleansing session took the whole morning. When we returned, they set to work on my face. They removed the hair from my face for the first time, using fine cotton. It was painful and I cried constantly. They shaped my eyebrows and made-up my face. They kept colouring my eyelashes, because tears kept washing the dye away.

'Everyone seemed happy, jubilant, except me, I was mourning my own death. They had been working on my dress for days, finally, when I tried it on, I could not control my tears, it felt to me like a shroud. "This is normal," they kept saying, "it is a big change in their lives." Mother occasionally burst into tears as well. They all assumed that this was natural, a mother letting go of her daughter, that was hard, and the daughter leaving the parents' home and to take on the big responsibility of having her own family, being initiated into adult life. "It is joy and pain, just like childbirth," I was told. "Without pain the birth does not come about."

'People came that day from all over the village and from neighbouring villages. Women gathered in our house and in next door house, all the menfolk were gathered, a third and fourth house were used for preparation of the food and refreshments, and so on.

'Here I was all made up and dressed up, seated in the middle of the room on a stool and all around me were the women sitting on the floor, the room was packed, they were all in their colourful best clothes. I looked around, I felt as if they had all come to my funeral. Occasionally they would turn around and throw handfuls of sweets and coins over my head and children would rush with excitement and jubilation to collect them, laughing.

'The night before mother pulled me into a corner for a word of advice, as she put it. "My dear daughter, I want to tell you what will happen on your wedding night and how you must cope with it. He will sleep with you, you must let him do whatever is necessary, he will know what to do. I must tell you that it will be a bit painful but it will be quick, the more you relax the easier and quicker it will be over. This, every woman has to go through." I kept weeping as she spoke and I could see that she was trying hard to keep her tears under control. "You just let him get on with it. Don't resist. The more you resist the more pain you will experience. Your role is to let him do as he wishes. It is a kind of leaving your body, you know, not to be aware of it, taking your mind off it for a little while, do you understand, my dear daughter? In this way you won't feel the pain of the penetration." Then she embraced me and we both cried, she shared my pain. I had made up my mind that I was not going to let him touch me at whatever cost, whatever happened he was not having me. In the end he would divorce me and then I would run away to where Morad was in the war zone, I would free myself.

'It was in the early evening that they came for me, to take me to Bahram's home, supposedly to my home. Mother and Aunt Masoomeh were to come with me, halfway, we would travel on a donkey to the place where I was to be met by Bahram who would take me on by his horse. I do not have much memory of what passed between us on the way, I just found myself in this room with him. I was dazed. Maybe I had escaped, maybe I had left my body as mother had said. Here we were, left in the room just the two of us, the door was closed upon the two of us. My heart started pumping as though I was coming to myself, I was dreading what would happen next. He came and sat beside me. I was holding the veil covering my face tightly. "Well, we are on our own now," he said, as though I wasn't aware. I kept quiet. After a little pause he said, "You don't have to hold the veil over your face so tight now, you know," he said with laughter. His voice repelled me, I could hear his heavy breathing, I hated him near me, I had my eyes closed.

'After a little while he said, "Khadijeh, we are husband and wife now." I kept silent. Then he asked if I wanted something to eat. I did not answer. Suddenly he laughed, "Don't you have a tongue, won't you talk to me? You needn't be so shy, I am your husband, you know, try to talk to me, take your veil off and let me see your beautiful face." He stretched out his hand, trying to loosen my tight grip on the cloth. I held it tighter and moved back. He did not expect this. I noticed the angry look on his face, but then he calmed down. He brought me a drink of sherbet, held the glass in front of me, "Take it and drink it, you'll feel better," he said with a shaky voice. "Come on, it's for you, take it, you haven't had anything to drink for some time." I did not respond. After a little while he drank it himself.

'After another pause he said, "How long do you want to sit there in silence?" I ignored his question. After a while he came and sat right beside me, his body nearly touching mine. I tried to move away but he grabbed my arm and held it tight. "You are not moving away from me, you are my wife, do you understand? Now you are my wife, we are married, I am your husband, I can do whatever I like with you now." And he laughed aloud. "It is not that day at the spring, you ignored me, do you remember?" With this he shook my arm, gripped it tighter, "Now I've got you, you are my wife, I can do whatever I feel like with you." With this, he held my hand tight. "And you know what I feel like tonight, don't you?" Another laugh. His voice repelled me, I felt the filth, violence, and cruelty in him, I smelt it, I tasted it. With one swift movement I pushed him aside freeing my arm and moved away from him right into a corner. I had pushed my elbow into him and this must have taken the wind out of him, he was stunned at my unexpected action.

'He came towards me like an angry dog, he slapped me and kicked me almost in one go. I did not cry or make any noise, I did not feel like giving him that satisfaction. He hit me again and again and again. He must have kicked my head against the wall, the blood started pouring from my nose, he kept on hitting me, kicking, punching. I tried to protect my head and chest with my arms and legs. "I'll show you what that means," he said raising his hand above me, "you little bitch, this will teach you a lesson. You thought I would let you get away with it, you must be dreaming. This should bring you to your senses." Blood was streaming down my face, my clothes were soaked. "Get out of here now, clean yourself, I don't want your nasty blood to get on the carpet. Out with you." With this he kicked me and dragged me towards the floor. He opened the door and pushed me out and closed the door behind.

'Mother and another woman, Akramkhanom, an aunt of his I think, were waiting outside to receive the virginity towels. They attended to me. I could see Aunt Masoomeh was crying. The other woman said to me, "It looks as though you have been disobedient. You'll learn, you are young." They cleaned me up and changed my clothes and forced me to drink some sherbet. Mother had said, "We are sure of our daughter, she has just been a little hardheaded, that's because she is young, she'll learn." They let me in again. I did not have my head cover on this time. "Oh that's better," he commented, "I can see your face now. It's a little bit swollen but it'll go down in time, it'll teach you not to be so obstinate, not with me anyway, you must know your place. I will not do that to you all the time, not unless you disobey me, then it'll be much more severe than this I assure you, this is nothing, you'll see. Come to bed now, it is bedtime, isn't it? It's very late." He was grinning, everything about him filled me with disgust.

'He grabbed my arm and dragged me towards the bed. At

the edge he said, "In order to get into this bed you have to take your clothes off first." I stopped and stiffened myself. "Come on, I'll help you." He tried to get my clothes off, he pulled, he pushed, he tore, he ripped, he broke. Once or twice he slapped me as I resisted. Once he had got everything off he said, "You have got a beautiful body, just as I imagined. Despite your obstinate mind and foul temper your body is beautiful but I shall tame you, it is your body I want now." Then he started undressing himself. I closed my eyes. Then he had his arms around me and was pulling me to bed. He was trying to flatten me. I bit his shoulder as hard as I could. He screamed and let go of me. Then I attacked. He was curled up holding his shoulder. I kicked him, punched him, bit him, hit him as hard as I could, spat on him. I wanted to kick him right between his legs, to crush his balls and his thingy. He had his legs curled in front of him. I was filled with energy, strength, force, there was no limit to this sudden burst of energy in me. Suddenly, Majan's experience was alive in my mind. I could see her, hear her, feel her being crushed and it was as though I was defending her, revenging her and all the other women who had been beaten and crushed. Father was there beating up mother. Mother's screams. Majan's screams. How they were being crushed. Suddenly I hated all men. I hated him. I wanted to kill him. Habib beating up me, and many other women I had heard of, all of them were alive for me now, they were all there in that room. The air was full of it. All those maidservants the landlords raped. I could hear their screams far away and nearby, different distances between, looking as though there were so many they stretched to the stars. It was as though all the energy of those women had come to me, I was bursting with energy, it was colossal, I felt strong and brave, wild with it and I wanted to hurt the men for everything they had done to all those women. Now I could show them what it was like to be crushed. It felt good to be giving them a taste of it.

'Bahram was trembling, shaking, he was like a wounded

tiger, growling, grunting. I gave him as much as I wanted to and I felt good, I felt on top and it felt good battering his naked body. And then I stopped. I looked at him, he looked pathetic, his body all bruised and bloody, his body trembling and shaking. I spat on his face and watched his helplessness. I felt at peace with myself, happy, as though I had got rid of a massive load from my shoulders, I felt light, triumphant, I felt good. And I left him in his shit. That was how he looked to me at that moment.

'I started putting on my clothes, suddenly he sprang up in a flash, took hold of a silver candle holder from the shelf and threw it straight at my head. I didn't feel anything for a few moments. Then I was on the floor, the room was going round and he was kicking me all over, then I did not feel anything. I felt as if my hands and legs were being tied up, then I was being dragged by my hair and then he was tying my hair round the leg of the chest. Then he threw himself on me, forcing my legs open, and I stiffened myself as hard as I could, as hard as metal.

'He was bashing around in my private parts with his thingy and kept on, then with his fist. He kept kicking my buttocks but I stiffened myself like a tree, I was hard as a rock. I screamed, I shouted, I swore, I gave one great yell with all my might, right from my stomach, it shook the whole house. It was said that that cry of mine was heard in the whole village. Ever since it has been referred to as "The night that Khadijeh yelled." It was said that it disturbed and alarmed the animals, the dogs, cats and donkeys had all shown signs of distress. It was said that I sounded like an animal. He threw cushions over my face. Suddenly he leapt towards me again and must have struck my head with the candlestick, after that I don't know what happened.

'When I came round mother was sitting next to me and holding my hand, apparently I had come round earlier and screamed my head off and then fallen unconscious again. I have no memories of that. For three days I lay in bed unaware of anything around me, I lay ill in bed for three months and have remained ill ever since. I would rather be ill than go back to him or someone else like him. This way was more comfortable, much more free. I was left alone. That was the only way. Many bones in my body had been broken, including my head in several places, and around my private parts. I don't know how I survived, people did not think I would. I don't know why I survived so long, I wish I was dead, it would have been a lot easier for everyone concerned, I have been a burden on the family. I've brought shame on the family. It is not fair, I know, but it was not my fault, but you see it was not my doing. I still see him in my nightmares. He is nude, his bits and pieces dangling as his body sways around this way and that, his eyes hanging out of their sockets, his face bewildered, a dagger in his hand aimed at my heart, his mouth wide open, his tongue hanging out, it has been slashed, his voice coming out of his ears, his body giving out some kind of poison, he is wretched, the sight of him is foul, he is ugly, he is revolting, he will cut me to pieces he says. Next it is me with the dagger in my hand, I throw it straight to his heart, cut off his flesh in pieces, I break his bones into bits, his blood runs, it runs more and more and more, the blood eventually loses its colour, then gradually I hear the voices of all those women, singing, clapping. I see them dancing, like shadows, praising, and I feel light, the same lightness I felt that night after battering him.

'I couldn't take on motherhood for the child that followed, I was only a vehicle for her to come through, she wasn't of my making, she would have intensified my memories of him, I could not have coped with that. He never set eyes on her, forsaken soul, I wondered what would become of her. I have always wondered this, how her life would evolve. She has come through me but she is not from me, I am not responsible for her plight, people come and go in this world as a result of mishaps in the course of things, it just happened that I was the vehicle for her coming.

'But in my dreams I still meet up with Morad, we are exactly the same as we were in those days, young, happy and full of life. We have a wonderful time together, we sing, we dance together, we laugh and we merge into each other. That was why I wanted to have my own place so that I could meet with him as often as I wanted. I do want to join him. I want to go with him. He is waiting for me. I can dream freely, I have my own space, that's all I have, my memories, and I want to indulge in them in my own space.'

She said a hearty goodbye to everyone when she left. 'It's a good to be going home, but I have a feeling I'll be back in Teheran before too long!' she announced.

Independence

After separating from her husband and then his subsequent death, Mahi lived for nearly a year with her brother, Ezatollah. She had been given the room next to the grocery shop. 'Do whatever you like,' her brother had said. 'Feel free to do exactly as you like.'

She normally ate with the family, they cooked and ate together, a large group, ten to twenty people at a time. They gave big parties and Mahi would be the main organiser of the catering and the entertainment. She carried out the important tasks of making jams and pickles, drying herbs, making tomato and pomegranate purees, preparing large quantities for winter, for the whole family. Mahi was also the family stylist – dressmaking, haircutting and special make-up were all done under her supervision, or with her help and advice.

Mahi was highly respected in the neighbourhood and by her family but this wasn't enough for her. It wasn't long before Mahi began feeling uncomfortable and restless about living in that house 'under my brother's shadow' as she put it. She lacked something fundamental, she felt, freedom, independence, being the master of herself. As she explained to her mother, 'I don't want to be a burden on my brother for the rest of my life because this is what I am at the moment, a burden. I want to earn my own living and live my own life, with a home of my own. I don't want someone else to have control over me. Here everything is cut out, determined, you just follow you don't create. I want to create new things, not just follow.'

'But how do you expect to cope? A young widow with three young children in this strange bewildering city, all on your own. How can you think of moving away from us? This is madness. You won't be able to survive without a man to look after you,' her mother Roghiieh reminded her.

'But I don't need a man to look after me. What do I want a man for? I am just as tough as a man, I am as capable as a man, what do I have less than a man? You just tell me what a man has that I have not,' she challenged her mother. 'I have worked, I have earned my living before, why can't I do it now? What is different now? What's more, I feel stronger now. Reza used to leave me months on end and go I don't know where on his travels and adventures and I had to look after the family single-handed.

'But that was in a village,' Roghiieh said, 'which is quite different from Teheran. There you had people looking after you, the whole community, but here, who would look after you? Here there are millions of people, all strangers, you don't know what kind of people you may come into contact with. You can't trust strangers.'

'Yes, but I also worked here, doing people's washing, don't you remember? Have you forgotten how I worked and supported the family when Reza couldn't find a steady job? I want to go back to that same area. I have some contacts there, former customers who would have me back again I am sure. They treated me well, they respected me. I am an honest and hardworking person, willing to do anything, I have been told many times I am a good worker and I am confident that I will manage to make my own living and will bring up my children on my own. Some of those people will either have me back or find me other families to work for.'

'But do you want to be a washerwoman for the rest of your life? What will people in the neighbourhood say if you do that kind of work? What will they think of us?'

'What's wrong with earning my living through my own labour? I will be doing honest work mother, do you understand? I am not soliciting, I am not doing anything immoral, if that is what you are frightened of. I won't bring shame on you.'

'Why can't you live with us and have a quiet, comfortable life here? You've got everything you want, no one has ever said anything to you to give you offence, what do you want to go for?'

'I told you, you don't seem to understand, you don't seem to hear me. I want to live my own life. I want to stand on my own feet, be my own mistress, bring up my family the way I want to. How many times do I have to say it so that you understand?'

'So you don't need us any more, is that what you are saying?' Roghiieh asked in exasperation.

'But I do need you mother. I'll come and visit you, and you can come and visit me, we will see each other often. It is only about an hour-and-a-half walk from here, it takes only half-an-hour with a horse-drawn car, it is not as though I were moving to the other end of the world. I want to have my own home.'

'Without a man?'

'Yes, without a man, mother,' Mahi shouted with anger.

'It is useless for us to talk, you are just as stubborn as your sister,' Roghiieh lost her temper. 'I don't know, do whatever you like, you will bring disgrace on yourself and us, just like your sister, it is no good trying to reason with you.'

'But what did my sister do wrong? She did nothing wrong. See how different she has been since she moved away from Habib's. He treated her brutally, but she has been happy since she left his house, and she is a lot better, isn't she? Mother, life isn't just having bread to eat and a place to sleep. It's more than that. Khadijeh didn't bring any disgrace on you and neither will I. I want my children to look at me and learn independence from me and respect me for the way I live. They have no father to learn from, so they must learn from me.'

'But you are a young woman, a widow, with three young children and a stranger to this city, you don't know their ways. You could be trampled upon, used, abused, destroyed, do you understand?'

'I am young, so what? Am I honey to be fingered and sucked? I have my own mind. I am strong. I can think. I can use my mind. I can judge. I can cope. I can look after myself, mother, for the last time I am telling you, I can look after myself. You treat me as though I am still a little girl and need to be chaperoned. I don't want to live under the shadow of my brother for the rest of my life.'

'What will people say?'

'To hell with people and what they say, I don't want my life to be controlled by what people say. That is your problem, mother, since you care so much about what people say. You stay with your people and their sayings, I'll be gone.'

With this, Mahi stormed out of the room, slamming the door hard. She wrapped her *chador* around her body, covering herself from head to foot, and went out of the house. She wouldn't be left alone in the house and she wanted to be on her own to think things over. So she walked the narrow streets and the alleyways of the neighbourhood. She walked for many hours until darkness fell. She covered her face tightly with the *chador* so as not to be recognised and avoided any familiar faces she came across.

Mahi walked on and on, aimlessly, talking to herself as she walked, sometimes coherently, sometimes deliriously. 'This is no good, I can't do it, I can't go on, I have failed yet again. There is no man to stand by me, watch over me, support me in times of need as mother says. None of my village friends around to stand by me. I am all alone with three young children in this vast city, I can't do it, I can't go on. This is no good, this life was not meant for me.' She was disturbed, disorientated, as a new plan formed in her mind.

She walked towards the shopping area and found the shop she wanted. She reached inside her *chador* and searched for the knotted corner of her scarf, which Mahi opened with shaking fingers. Yes, she had some money, it would be enough. Mahi entered the shop and asked for opium, paid and left quickly, hoping no one she knew had seen her. 'This life was not meant for me,' she thought. 'Things will be better next time round. I am sure this is the best way out of it, I'll be at peace, so will everyone else concerned.' She held the opium tight, the cube-like piece felt good in her hand. She must keep it safe, she felt secure just holding it. It was wrapped in a piece of paper. She opened it, smelled it, yes, it was the right stuff, and a good piece too, about an inch in length. She put it back in the paper and wrapped it in the corner of her scarf and knotted it, the same corner where she kept those coins for an emergency, and this was an emergency, the most pressing one she could have saved them for.

Mahi walked back, entered the house discreetly, went to her room, threw herself on the bed. 'I am not well,' she said to her enquiring, anxious children, 'find what you can in the house and eat, I'll be better tomorrow, you'll be better too,' she mumbled in a shaky voice. She covered her head and groaned. She talked to herself, deliriously, 'Hey, who is there? Is that you? I am coming, wait for me, I'm coming, it's over.' She would laugh occasionally, feverishly.

It was midnight, and Mahi managed to crawl out to get herself a drink of water. She released her grip on the knotted corner of her scraf. It was time now to open it. The knot was tight and her fingers were trembling. It took a bit of doing, opening it. She put the lump in her mouth, picked up the bowl of water, took a big mouthful, put her head back and with one action swallowed it down. 'There, I've done it.' Then she crawled back to bed and laid down. 'This is it, no more suffering now. The children will grow up whether I am here or not. I might be doing them more damage the way I am now. I have been unlucky all my life. How bad of me to argue with mother, I upset her, by answering back. I know I shouldn't but I always do, I can not hold my tongue. 'Your tongue needs to be cut off,' she used to say to me. It is all over now, mother, I won't answer you back or argue with you, not any more. Forgive me mother. It will be better next time around.' Then her voice stopped, her eyes felt heavy and she sank into unconsciousness.

Mahi was still unconscious when her children found her the next morning. Frightened and crying, they woke the adults. Her family, very distressed, took her to the hospital. Her stomach was washed out. She was saved, just about. Some weeks later, having recovered from the overdose, she had a serious talk with her brother, Ezat. Ezat had said to her in the past, 'You had better stay put here with us, it is in your best interest and ours, we would be worried about you, what would people say? If you went people would say that I did not look after you and let you loose in this strange city with the children, I would be held responsible and I would never forgive myself if anything happened to you.' But on this occasion his attitude was different. For he had realised the strength of his sister's desire to move away, to be independent. The suicide bid had made this very clear to all the family.

'I thank you, brother, for your concern and generosity having looked after us all this time but it is time, I feel, for me to move away, to have my own life. I want to stand on my own feet, I want to earn my own living. I'll manage I assure you and I won't get into a mess which might cause you embarrassment, shame, I promise. I believe in my own strength, just give me the chance to prove it. This is crucial for me, this would give a meaning to my life, being independent, useful. I like challenges in life. I need to discover a sense of my own worth. At the moment I feel I am wasting away, I feel a burden upon you and the rest of the family. You need to build your own life, you are taking care of too many people. You are in your mid-thirties now, still not married, because of all these responsibilities you create for yourself.'

'How far do you want to go? You leaving wouldn't make any difference,' Ezat said calmly.

'Four less people to be responsible for. But this would give a purpose to my life, a direction. You don't want me to waste away, do you? I know I can live here with you for the rest of my life, be comfortable, have no worries for food, for tomorrow. Here you send my youngest child to school, you oversee his education, pay for his schooling, help him with his homework every day, but you have to consider me as well, this is at some cost to me. I get demoralised and become ill, this is no good for my children, I am no good to anyone. I took that opium because I felt my life had no meaning, no direction, no purpose, I was too depressed, I need an aim in my life, do you understand, brother?'

Then a long silence fell between them. Ezat had listened to her patiently and was chewing over what she had said. 'Do whatever you feel is right,' he said finally. 'You need to be happy. I can't keep you here by force, I can only offer you my advice, you are free to take it or leave it. I can say what I think is right for you but if you don't agree and want to do as you please, then I cannot force it upon you. You do whatever you think fit but just tell me one thing, what is wrong with living here?'

'Nothing is wrong with living here. You have all been very kind to me.'

'But has anyone said anything which has offended you?'

'No, brother, no one has said anything to me.'

'Right, there is nothing left for me to say then. Do

whatever you like.' And with this he left the room with a look of great sadness on his face.

The next day Mahi left the house in the morning and was away for the whole day, she walked all the way there, about an hour-and-a-half walk, to Sarsabil where she had lived before, to see Mash Ihia, he was the right person to see, he was sure to help. An acquaintance had told Reza about Mash Ihia before they left the village. He had heard of Mash Ihia's reputation from distant relatives who had met him and had received help from him. 'You just have to remember two things,' Reza had been told, 'Mash Ihia and the area called Sarsabil, anyone for miles around that area will point him out to you.' He helped everyone, no one going to see him came back empty-handed, he attended to everyone's problems. He was called Moshgelgosha, as a nickname, opener and solver of problems.

When they had arrived in Teheran Reza had managed to find Mash Ihia quite easily. He had found them a place to live and later on, when Mahi separated from her husband, it was Mash Ihia who had discovered Reza's illness and had alerted Mahi. It was he who had found washing jobs for Mahi with families in the area.

He seemed to know everyone, it was as though the world knew him. He was a small, old man, though no one knew how old, or anything about his past, where he had come from, what kind of background he had had, his family circumstances, all this was a mystery. Sometimes he seemed almost ageless. Some people had known him for forty years or more and swore he had hardly changed during this time. He walked everywhere, taking small steps, walking fast, dragging his sandalled feet, summer and winter. Even in the most severe winter he never wore much warm clothing.

Mash Ihia lived in a tiny room, it was said, though no one had ever seen it. He never cooked for himself, and never spent any money on food or clothing. He never got ill and always ate at other people's homes. He laughed a lot, heartily, so hard at times that it almost seemed the earth shook. He knew everybody and all their secrets. The women joked, if you were pregnant, Mash Ihia would know first.

He told stories, endless stories he knew, it was said that you never heard his stories twice. He told anecdotes, recited poems. He could not read and write but he was full of stories, history, and he was full of facts and information about anything and everything you wished to name, he could give you a comprehensive knowledge of it and he could talk non-stop, indefinitely it seemed. He did not know tiredness. Everyone trusted him and he had a special relationship with women, they never hesitated to talk about anything in his presence, no secrets were kept from him.

He would appear suddenly from nowhere on people's doorsteps at any time, but especially at mealtimes! He wouldn't come in, he would sit just by the door and would gratefully receive a bowl of whatever they were going to have, eat it up, exchange the day's gossip and leave, just like that. He was always smiling, laughter never left him, that was what characterised him and set him apart from the rest of the population, this constant laughter and telling of jokes.

He had detailed knowledge of everyone's life. Who had had an affair with whom and for how long. Who was not a virgin on their wedding night. Everyone brought their troubles to him, he would listen patiently then offer advice and console them, tell them a few jokes and get them laughing until they were beside themselves. He was so free in his interaction with people. He was a child with a child, woman with a woman, and man with a man.

Mahi found Mash Ihia that day at the garage joking and chatting with the garage attendant. She had a good talk with him and told him what she was looking for, 'A room somewhere in this area for me to live in, and a family to work for.'

'Leave it with me, lady,' he said with hope in his eyes, 'don't you worry, leave it to me, I'll let you know, I know just the thing you are after. Now, go home and be happy.'

Mahi felt revived, renewed after the meeting with him, a new hope filled her, she felt happy. She called on a few of her old clients and enquired if there were any vacancies. A couple of them said they would gladly have her back on a weekly basis but they did not know of a vacant room. In the afternoon she continued knocking on doors in the area. 'Have you got a vacant room?' Either they did not have one or they couldn't risk taking on a single woman with three young children, not being sure if she could pay the rent. 'No, sorry, we are not sure about a room yet,' some of them had replied when in fact they did have a vacant room.

She came home in the evening, feeling tired, but still happy, hopeful, she had complete trust in Mash Ihia just as she had complete trust in herself, in her abilities. She went to the area every few days and looked around, making enquiries. She walked all the way there and back, long walks, taking a couple of hours each way but she preferred to do that than ask for the fares from her brother.

Some weeks passed. One day she was pickling aubergines, for the coming winter, in great big earthenware pots. As usual such tasks were on a large scale because of the non-stop stream of visitors that came and stayed in the house. Suddenly she heard the familiar laughter and voice of Mash Ihia, 'I need to see her, I am a messenger with a good message.' He told her that he had found somewhere for her to live and some work for her to do. It sounded like a miracle to Mahi. 'The daughter of someone I know, got married recently and they are now living in a house with a vacant room. The owner of the house who lives downstairs has just divorced his wife and has moved to one room and is renting the other room, and the two rooms upstairs are occupied by this couple who are looking for someone to help with the housework especially now that the lady is expecting.'

111

'This seems too good to be true,' Mahi exclaimed excitedly, 'accommodation and work, all in one place.'

Mahi moved to her new home within days. It was a nice little room, a back room, but she didn't mind that. She did all the housework for the lady upstairs, and she found some regular jobs outside as well, building up a good circle of clients. Mahi's family did not help her move or settle in. Indeed, they did not speak to her for nearly a year afterwards. But now the New Year was approaching and Mahi was busy spring-cleaning. She felt happy, full of energy, she was singing as she worked away, putting all the furniture outside. She was washing, cleaning, airing, she was going to decorate the room. She had been shopping the day before and had bought a new samovar. She was thrilled, as it was the first samovar she had owned since living in Teheran. She had been making do with a small tin kettle up until then. 'Tea will taste differently in my house from now on,' she said to herself.

She had brought some material to make new clothes for the children for *Norooz*. New clothes for the children were a necessity at this time of year, and she felt proud at having managed to earn the money to do that. Those long hard-working days were all worthwhile, she smiled to herself. She was sure that at *Norooz* her family would come to her and take her back. It was bound to happen. Reunion, acceptance, apologies, forgiving and forgetting. This was what *Norooz* was all about, starting anew.

'How proud they will be of me, seeing how well I have managed. My children are well looked after. I have proved once more that I am capable. They will respect me more for it. Mother and Ezat will both be proud of me. I have not brought shame on them after all. They were only concerned for my welfare. Poor mother, she never had to work and earn her own living, she has always depended on men, father, husband and now son, for her livelihood. She cannot imagine how a woman can earn her own living and take care of her family. She can see now that I have done it.

She will be pleased to see my home, and new belongings, all carefully chosen. I have got so much to show her and I have earned it all through the work of my own two hands. What a reunion we'll have on *Norooz* Day!' Mahi sighed contentedly, knowing in her heart that this was all to come.

Mash Ihia, Problem-solver

One day Mash Ihia called on Mahi unexpectedly. After giving her the usual detailed rundown of local news (this was one of the things that he did, spread the news, he was even known as the local newsman) he announced, 'But I have special news for you today, Mahi.'

'What is that?' Mahi asked, her eyes sparkling.

'Well, you remember Hussein, don't you?' he said and studied her face as he asked the question. Mahi blushed and dropped her head quickly, she wiped the sweat from her forehead with the corner of her scarf. 'Yes, you do remember! He has asked me to ask you if you will marry him.' Then he laughed heartily, which made Mahi laugh too. 'In other words, on his behalf, I have come here to ask for your hand.' He paused for a moment. 'Well, what do you say to that, heh?' and then laughed again. 'He is a good man as you know.'

Mahi had met Hussein soon after moving to Teheran. When Reza and Mahi first arrived in the city they stayed with her family for a little while until they found their own place. Reza was anxious not to stay with them more than absolutely necessary because he did not feel comfortable with them.

Mash Ihia had found them a basement room on a corner of a garage in South Teheran some eight kilometres away from where Mahi's family lived. A few days later they moved in.

One early morning Mahi had got up to say her prayer before sunrise and Reza had left to join the queue in the square where the contractors came to pick the local labourers for the day. When her prayer was finished, Mahi busied herself with tidying up and organising things in the little room which housed their family of six, the youngest a baby one year old. After a while she looked for a match to light the stove to boil water for tea. The matchbox was empty. Surely she could borrow a match in the neighbourhood somewhere she thought to herself, and with that thought she ventured out.

Bright sunshine streamed into the room as she opened the door and a fresh morning breeze stroked her cheeks as she climbed up the stairs. This was the first time she had stepped out into Teheran on her own, she was excited. She stood on the pavement at the top of the stairs and looked round. So many cars and lorries going by, so many people going in every direction, all different colours and sizes and shapes. She stood there for some moments just watching, mesmerised. If only Khoshghadam was here to share all this with me, she said to herself, I have so much to tell her.

She looked around for a house or somewhere she could ask for a match, then she noticed a shop behind her right above her basement room, inside were papers and books and magazines. She went in. A tall, dark man was standing behind the counter. She greeted him with a smile.

'Excuse me, do you think I could borrow a match from you?' she said with a shyness in her voice.

'What was that?' he said in Farsi, with a smile, and then they both laughed.

'A match,' she repeated, at the same time making a gesture of striking a match with her fingers and blowing fire. He laughed heartily, he was amused. She laughed too.

He understood and handed her a box of matches. She took it and pointing to the basement she said, 'I live down there, I'll bring it back in a minute,' and with that she walked out and down the stairs.

She lit the stove and took back the matches. 'Thank you,' she said in Turkish, with a broad smile, handing the matchbox to him.

'No, you can keep it,' he said, 'please,' gesturing that she should take it back and Mahi insisting that he should have it back. Then with a laugh he took the matchbox from her, emptied half of it into his hand and gave her the box half-filled with matches.

'No, I have a box, you give me the other half,' she said, gesturing with her hands at the same time. He understood and gave her the matches without the box. 'Thank you,' she said, looking him in the face. It was then that their eyes met. Mahi felt the thrill of instant attraction and her heart raced. She blushed, and he saw it. 'Thank you,' she stammered quietly as she walked out. He just looked, his eyes following her out, he felt nailed to the spot.

From that moment on she tried to get a glimpse of him whenever she could. She listened for his footsteps in the shop, she recognised them, his footsteps had definition, strength, purpose, it gave her assurance and made her happy. Each time they met he winked at her, they both smiled, sometimes she winked back as though they were reminding each other of a secret between them. It was the highlight of her day the moments they interacted, even a glance or a smile which she managed to steal excited her. At times she felt he waited for her, positioning himself so that she could catch a glimpse of him. Soon they got to know each other's movements and signals.

Eventually Reza became aware of these glances and smiles and the change in his wife, she was bubbly, full of life and energy. 'Is she pregnant?' he wondered. In pregnancy she behaved like that but he could not remember when last they made love. Mahi hated having sex with him, she would do anything to escape it, to put him off she would swear at him, cursing him, and he would plead.

Soon she gleaned some information about her neighbour by eavesdropping. His name was Hussein, he had been in that shop for a good few years, he loved books, he read a lot, he was knowledgeable, an intellectual, and he did not have a wife. He was respected in the neighbourhood. How she longed to talk to him, she worked even harder at learning Farsi, not knowing that he was learning Turkish in order to communicate with her. He had thick black hair, large black eyes and each time she saw his face it revealed so much to her about him. Those eyes, how they penetrated her, consumed her. He held his head high and laughed a lot, heartily and often.

Reza felt uncomfortable and agitated when Hussein was around, it was very noticeable. Hussein made his presence felt and Reza became suspicious. All these mood changes in Mahi, she became dreamy and withdrew from Reza even more. His discomfort grew as the days went by especially as he was at home much of the time, unable to get a job. Occasional casual labour came up for him, but that was all, generally he was around. Hussein and Mahi's fondness for each other grew, as did Reza's suspicion and anxiety.

Reza became sulky and miserable, looking for an excuse to get at Hussein until one morning the door was open and the sun streamed through, fresh air filling the room, Mahi poured the tea and handed it to Reza, stirring it. As she turned there he was on top of the stairs looking at her, smiling, and Mahi smiled back. Reza saw it all. That was it. He went into a rage, threw the glass full of tea at the stairs and stood up. 'What are you grinning for?' he shouted at his wife, 'and what do you think you are doing, Mister, staring into my house at this hour of the morning?' He climbed the stairs quickly. 'What is it that you want from us, heh? Why don't you leave us alone?' he shouted at the top of his voice, his voice shaking, 'With all those dirty looks of yours, you filthy, immoral man!' Hussein went back to his shop. Reza followed him and slapped him, then came running back down the stairs.

Hussein came again, shouting in Turkish, 'Come out here, if you are a man, I'll show you what that means. I don't want to come down there in front of your family, you come up here,' he shouted with a strong voice, then he reverted to Farsi, repeatedly challenging him to come up. 'I don't want to come down there where your family is, come up here and I'll show you. You come up here and face me if you are a man.'

'You dare lift a hand to me,' Reza said. 'Do you think I haven't noticed your dirty looks, you corrupt, immoral man?'

'Only out of respect for your family I am not coming down there. You don't deserve them by the way.'

Mahi gently asked Ali, who was near the door, to close it.

That very morning Reza started searching for a new place to live and within a few days he had found one and moved the family out. From that time on they didn't speak to each other again, Reza and Mahi, not properly. They would give messages to each other through their children. Mahi was furious with him for having treated Hussein in that manner and Reza was heartbroken, humiliated, and his health started going rapidly downhill. He stopped eating and depression set in. It was quite normal for them to go days without even speaking to each other at all. The relationship between them went from bad to worse and soon reached breaking point.

One day Mahi went to work as usual in the morning. She walked for half-an-hour to get to the first job, but just before reaching the house where she was expected to do the washing, she suddenly found herself face to face with Hussein. For a moment her heart stopped. 'That's right, it's me,' Hussein said with a gentle, quiet voice yet strong and determined. 'I just wanted to see you, Mahi,' he said in

Turkish. He had learned Turkish, Mahi couldn't believe her eyes or ears.

'You know my name,' she said in Farsi. 'You've learned Farsi,' he said. 'And you've learned Turkish.' They both laughed heartily, hysterically. Then both stopped and complete silence fell between them for a moment or two. This meeting was a shock to her system. She had not expected to see him like that on her own, in a different area. Suddenly she felt the world existed just for them, no one else mattered. In a flash, she felt a sense of oneness with him, she felt complete. She closed her eyes, taking the thought of him deep inside her. How she had longed for this moment, and she felt they were floating together, far away from the everyday world. It filled her with joy.

'Mahi, are you with me? Mahi, are you with me?' It was his voice.

'I am with you all the time,' said her laughing eyes.

'Look, I only wanted to talk with you just once, I promise I won't follow you any more if you don't want me to.'

The sweetness of his voice nourished her. She remained silent, taking in everything about him, his voice, his smell, the sight of him, she breathed the whole of him in.

'I am sorry about that day,' he was speaking in Turkish to her now. 'I promise I won't disturb you any more, I just wanted to tell you this, I just wanted to see you again.' Mahi made a silent gesture. They just looked at each other, for some moments they were together, right inside, together as one. They held each other. 'I'll be there always, always, always, whenever you need me.' Then she turned away from him, gesturing him to go before knocking on the door and did not look behind her when the door was opened.

She felt enriched that day, nourished, it felt as though she had known him for a very long time, perhaps because in many ways, he reminded her of her childhood sweetheart. He awakened the same intense feelings in her . . . could it be the same person, she wondered.

That day after work she walked home slowly, walking around quite a bit before reaching home. Reza questioned her suspiciously about her being late. Where had she been, who with? That made Mahi angry. 'What are you accusing me of?' she shouted, and a furious argument followed. That did it, she made her decision there and then, packed a few things, took the children and left the house. They were going to uncle's house, she told the children. On the main road they got into a horse-drawn cart, she paid their fares out of the money she had earned that very day.

The next morning she returned with her brother, Ezatollah, announcing that she was separating. 'I cannot live a life of suspicion and interrogation.' Reza knew that once she had made up her mind nothing would stop her, her brother knew this too. Reza was in tears, pleading with Mahi, begging her brother not to take her away, but to no effect, and Mahi was determined to leave. Ezat kept silent. Soon she was packed, ready. They left as Reza looked on in great sadness and with a heavy heart.

Mahi had not seen Hussein since that day when she had finally decided to leave Reza, although she had often thought of him. And now she must decide whether or not to accept his proposal. Mash Ihia had sat quietly by her side, while she was lost in her thoughts and memories. Suddenly he looked her straight in the face and said, 'Listen, you are not a teenager and this is not your first marriage and you are not being forced into it by your parents as I suspect you were with your other marriage.'

'Yes,' Mahi replied, 'I see that.'

'And he loves you, I can tell that and I believe you have feelings for him too. Am I right?' She kept silent. 'Mahi, what are you thinking about? Share your thoughts with me,' Mash Ihia said. 'I have been waiting in silence whilst you are in your own world. Share it with me.'

'I am sorry,' Mahi apologised.

'Well, think about it, you don't have to rush into a decision. It is in your interest if you marry, and if you

120

marry someone like him who loves you. You see, you are young, and alone in this strange town with three children. You have left your family, your mother and brothers I mean. He will make a good husband for you, I see it in his eyes, and I think he will make a good father for your children too. His wife died a few years back, and he has never had children of his own, so he will have to learn to be like a father. He is a learned man, he loves books, poetry, he writes poetry too. And he can recite poetry in Turkish too, he has learned Turkish recently.' He grinned looking at her with his eyes fixed upon her.

'I have to think about it, Mash Ihia,' she said, lifting her head and looking him in the face.

'Yes, of course. You think about it, but I advise you to accept it, it is in your interest I assure you, and I wouldn't say anything if I didn't feel it, you know that, don't you?'

'Yes, I know. And thank you for your concern for me.'

'I'll call next week at this time. Let me know if you want to talk to me before next week, you know where I am, don't you?' he said.

'I can't bring myself to accept, Mash Ihia, I have three young children, I can't take the responsibility of putting them at the mercy of a stepfather, how would he treat them? I would never forgive myself if he mistreated them. How could I live with myself?'

'But he may not mistreat them.'

'But the chances are that he may. You see, I have just found my freedom and independence, I am in control of my life now. It has taken me a long time with long battles to get here, I don't want to lose it. I am earning my living, I am managing my children, my life all right. I suppose it could be better, but we are doing fine. My older son, Ali, has taken an apprenticeship to learn to be a tailor. My younger son, Akbar, is in school and he is doing well, I am managing to pay for his schooling, so far anyway. And my daughter, well, I hope there will be an opening for her. God is great, something will come up for her I know, she will manage her own life. I don't know what yet but I am sure something is bound to come her way, fate will ensure that.'

'Yes, but what about you?' Mash Ihia said, thoughtfully.

This sent Mahi back into her thoughts again. 'I must admit that I haven't been lucky in my marriages, maybe that's my fate, maybe I never will be happy in marriage, maybe I have to accept it.' She immediately bit her tongue. Marriages, she did not mean to say it in the plural. She did not like to talk about her first marriage to anyone, it just popped out. Mash Ihia was looking at her, he understood but did not refer to it.

'Not been lucky? Well, you are not the only one whose husband has died while you are still young. Many marriages break up for one reason or another, but you can't keep yourself a prisoner of the past. The past is gone. You can determine the future, only so far though. Things don't repeat themselves all the time you know.' Then he left just as suddenly as he had appeared. This was his way, suddenly appearing from nowhere and then just as suddenly disappearing.

Mahi felt very lonely, she longed to have someone to share it with. If only she could talk it through with Khoshghadam. Now, there was no one with whom she could share it, there was no way in which she could discuss it with her newly made friends. There was so much of her own past that Khoshghadam was aware of and understood, how could she explain these things to anyone else? She felt the loneliness acutely, the isolation and deprivation. All the things she had gained in Teheran now stood in the balance against what she had lost, Khoshghadam, two marriages that had failed. What made her believe that a third one would be otherwise? Yet, she longed to be with him. She desired him, dreamt of him, how she wished he would take her in his strong arms and press her into him to become part of him when she felt weary of her burdens.

She dreamt of being with Khoshghadam and telling her how much she missed her and sharing with her all her excitement and this new prospect now that she was in love and that she was loved. She dreamt of Hussein, she dreamt of her childhood sweetheart, as they became one, moved from one to the other, merged into one, and Khoshghadam and herself, all layers as one. Now she had become more dreamy than ever, losing touch with reality at times and sensing danger, her responsibilities, her children, she had to be in one piece. In desperation she thought of turning her to her family for support. 'Didn't we tell you you would not be able to manage on your own?' her mother's voice rang in her ears.

She felt strongly that she should say yes to Hussein and marry him but the thought of her children being harmed by their stepfather froze her. 'What if I take the children and go back to the village and Khoshghadam, away from all this?' But the thought of the landlord alone was enough to send shivers down her spine.

She did not sleep for many nights and if she dozed off she woke suddenly from horrendous nightmares, all sweaty and frightened, she would pace up and down in the yard all night. If only she could be with Khoshghadam for a few days, if she could secretly visit her or bring her here but it seemed as impossible to reach her as reaching out to the stars. She sent messages to her whenever she could to come and visit her, pleading with messengers to deliver the message urgently, but she did not come.

I have no restrictions on me now, Khoshghadam, I am so free, I am mistress of my own, no one to tell me to come late or early, to wear this, do this or do that, to laugh or not laugh, no one to watch me, no one to criticise me, no one against me. The freedom I have now I would not exchange for the whole world. I am earning my own living. I do as I please, I am in charge of my own destiny, I decide everything that affects my life and the lives of my children. I cannot tell you how good it feels. No one to dictate to me, to control me. No landlords here. Then Mahi would wake with great disappointment and realise how far she was from her friend. How things had changed now that she was so close to her family and yet so far from them and so far from Khoshghadam. The independence she had gained stood in the balance with her desire to marry Hussein. Her dreams became much more intense, lengthy and frequent. She developed a severe fever for three days but she would not agree for her family to be told of this. Dreams of Hussein, the pleasure, the excitement with him, of her family taking her back, admiring her, respecting her, how she had managed, being proud of her. She moved between dreams and nightmares and sleeplessness.

It was Tuesday, Mash Ihia had said he would come back for an answer. Mahi got up early in the morning before sunrise as usual. After having said her prayer, she started the housework. It was her turn today to sweep the yard, the three women who lived in the house took turns to do it. Each day one of them would do the sweeping and cleaning. With a small brush she bent down and swept the whole yard, it was a large yard with a pond in the middle and flower beds round it, paved all along. It took a good hour to sweep it all including the staircase, the hallway and out the front, watering the flowers, clearing up as she went. Then Mahi left for the market to get her shopping. When she returned, the children were waking up. She gave them breakfast then left for work. She had to go to two households that day to do their washing. She came home late that afternoon, she felt shattered, but after a short rest she would be filled with renewed energy, she knew that, ready again to work, cooking, sewing, mending, cleaning and would work late into the night.

That evening she sat outside in the front alleyway with the other women of the neighbourhood, as she often did, mending her children's clothes. She had to be careful with the clothing as she could not afford to buy new ones often and she would alter them, patch them up to make them last that much longer. Sometimes the ladies for whom she worked gave their children's clothing to her, which she would alter to fit her children, and this evening she was altering a pair of those trousers to fit Akbar. The women chatted as they worked away, while the children played football nearby. Some of the women brought refreshments, and they cracked melon, pumpkin and water melon seeds which they had collected, cleaned, dried and roasted.

Mash Ihia arrived early that evening and after a cup of tea, he broached the subject. 'Well, Mahi, what is the news, what have you got to tell me? I hope I'm going to hear a "yes" answer because I would like to attend a wedding,' and he laughed heartily. 'Well, little princess, I am waiting.'

'I have to be honest with you, Mash Ihia.'

'You can't be otherwise. I can see through you,' Mash Ihia said, laughing loudly.

'I have thought about what you said last week. I can't bring myself to go through with this. I can't lose my independence. I can't take the responsibility for the effect on my children, so the answer has to be no.'

'I understand, don't try to explain. With all the restraints and restrictions you are faced with, and the experiences you've had, I'm not surprised that you have decided to say no.' The way he spoke it was as if he knew all about her life.

'To be honest with you, I can't make up my mind. I don't know exactly what I want. I don't know what is best for me under the circumstances.'

'All right, I'll tell him just that. That shows that you have some feelings towards him which will please him and he will appreciate that. You just take your time and whenever it feels right to you, then you will make a decision. You just see how things develop as time goes on. The right thing will occur to you. Come and see me whenever you want to talk about it. Or, send a message to him and talk with him.'

'To him?' Mahi said quickly.

'Of course, you two should meet and talk about it, you are both fully grown adults, you are not youngsters, a frank talk will do you both good. You should tell him your concerns and reasons, he will respect that, understand and appreciate that, I assure you. If you don't want to meet him alone, I can arrange a meeting for you. I'll be there, then people can't talk, can they?' he laughed. Anything Mash Ihia spoke about became humorous in the end, even if he talked about death, somehow towards the end he made it funny and everyone laughed. He laughed a great deal all the time. He left Mahi that evening with a huge sense of relief that she had been understood. She thought about Mash Ihia's suggestion that she should meet with Hussein on her own. It was an exciting idea, one she hoped some day to make into reality.

Ezatollah's Wedding

Ezatollah, Mahi's middle brother was now in his early thirties and still not married. 'It is time now for you to get married,' his mother kept reminding him. 'There is much talk about it amongst the families and neighbours. "When will Ezat marry?" they all ask.'

'Married? What do I want to get married for? You got married and what did you achieve? My sisters got married and look at them? I am married to my family, that is enough for me. Perhaps one day I will marry, but not now.'

Ezat was an ambitious young man, always wanting to improve the living conditions for all his family, so whenever there was talk of his marrying he deferred it to the future saying he had a lot more to do yet.

After years of working in Teheran, he had bought himself a large strip of land and built his own house. It took two years to complete. When it was finished his family had moved in. The main house was built at one end of the land, with two rooms on the ground floor, one either side of a large hallway. The first floor was identical with the addition of a large balcony at the front. At the other end of the piece of land he built two rooms with a cellar underneath, turning one of the rooms into a grocery shop for his brother Hasan, with an opening from outside.

The space between the two buildings he turned into a beautiful garden with a large pool in the middle, surrounded by stone paving, with flower beds stretching around the pool decorated with a zig-zag stone edging. He gradually planted many bushes, shrubs, plants such as cotton wool, and flowers of many kinds including roses, jasmine, geraniums, tulips and daffodils. The colours and the scent filled the air. He took a particular interest in his garden, it was his passion.

But despite his achievements, the women in his family felt something was missing from his life, and had been on the look out for a suitable girl for Ezat for some time. 'No more nonsense of "later",' Roghiieh put it strongly one day, 'I think we have found just the girl for you. Her name is Esmat, a Turkish girl. Her parents are coming to visit us on Friday for lunch, so you have to be home.'

Esmat had been visiting her aunt who had just moved to the area. A neighbour, Halimehkhanom had seen her and, knowing that they were looking for a girl for Ezat, had told them about her. 'She is a striking, beautiful girl, with a lovely personality. She is about sixteen or seventeen years old. She has long black, thick hair and large, black eyes. And her face is never without a smile.'

So it was that enquiries had started. Halimehkhanom found out, in a subtle manner through the aunt, where the girl lived, and whether she was engaged or not. Her parents lived quite a distance away, on the outskirts of Teheran, in Karadj. 'Couldn't you find someone nearer, mother?' Ezat joked.

'A good girl from a good family is worth going to the end of the world for, my son,' Roghiieh said in a serious tone.

'Where did you find this girl, mother?' Ezat asked with curiosity.

'Well, Halimehkhanom our neighbour met her in Nargeskhanom's house, she is a niece to Fatemehkhanom who recently moved next door to Nargeskhanom. She had just popped over to do Nargeskhanom's hair.'

'So she is a hairdresser, eh? A fashionable woman by the sound of it.'

'There is nothing wrong in a girl having every skill she can.'

After Halimehkhanom told them about Esmat, Mahi and her aunt Ghadamkhir had decided to pay her a preliminary visit. They set off early one morning, and had to change buses several times with long walks in between, on their journey to her home town. They had not been there before but they were confident of finding it. They had made these sorts of visits a few times before, none of which had been successful. Either the girl had not been suitable, or the family had not been good to deal with. And of course Ezat wasn't prepared to consider marriage, so they could not have managed to convince him anyway.

By the time they found the house it was early afternoon. They knocked and a beautiful young girl opened the door. She had a lovely face and was smiling at them. 'Is your mother home?' Ghadamkhir asked. The young girl's eyes twinkled as though she understood the whole thing and foresaw what was coming. Mahi giggled at her response.

'No,' she replied, smiling. 'She has just popped over to see my aunt, she won't be a minute, please come in.' The women entered. She led them to the front room. The women took off their shoes and walked in. She made sure that they were seated comfortably and then brought them tea, then a bowl of fruit which she offered round.

'Has your mother been gone long?' Ghadamkhir asked.

'Will she be long?' added Mahi. They were trying to make conversation with her and the two women carefully observed her responses, her movements and her behaviour.

'I'll go and tell her to come in a moment,' she said, shyly. 'It won't take me a minute, I'll be right back,' she said as she left the room.

It wasn't long before both mother and daughter returned. Esmat's mother welcomed Mahi and Ghadamkhir profusely. Both mother and daughter had already guessed the purpose of the strange women's visit. Any household with a daughter of that age could expect occasional visits such as this. Their conversation flowed easily. How long had the family lived here? Where had they come from? How old was the girl? They had already found out that she was not engaged. The women stayed for about an hour. The girl came in once more bringing tea, and a little while afterwards they left.

'Yes, this seems quite an attractive possibility. The girl is beautiful, her manners and behaviour are excellent, and they are a good family,' Mahi reported. The family discussed it thoroughly and told Ezat of their findings. It was agreed that they would send a message suggesting that a small group visit in a week's time for a preliminary talk.

That day, Roghiieh, Mahi, Ghadamkhir and Uncle Mamad-Ali called round. They took a photograph of Ezat to show Esmat's family. Her aunt and uncle were present as well as her parents. They talked about Ezat and gave details of his profession, age, family members, lifestyle, who lived with him, and so on. Then they asked the girl's parents if they would like to visit them. They agreed and set a date, on Friday, in two weeks time, for lunch.

The Friday visit, with Ezat present, came and went, satisfactorily. Then a meeting was arranged for the business side of the marriage. Both parties had to discuss and work out the conditions. A few of the senior members of the family of each side were involved in this. It was agreed that she would get 250,000 *rial* if he divorced her, but if she divorced him she would not be entitled to anything. Her family were given 50,000 *rial* in cash for the wedding expenses. Negotiations went smoothly. The meeting lasted a good few hours, but as both sides were quite keen on the prospect of the marriage no problems arose and when it was finished all seemed to be satisfied and happy with the arrangements. They would be engaged in a few weeks time, and the wedding would be in three months time in early autumn.

Ezat and Esmat met for the first time in the girl's house after her parents had been to lunch at Ezat's house. The door opened, Esmat entered, carrying a tea tray. She was wearing a brightly coloured, flowery frock and a pretty blue silk scarf on her head but her long, black hair was hanging over her shoulders in plaits with a thick fringe. She was petite and looked strong spirited. She had rosy cheeks and large laughing black eyes. Mahi noted how confident and self-assured she looked. First she offered tea to Mamad-Ali and Ghadamkhir, then to Ezat who was sitting next to Mahi. She was bending down, with the tray in front of him. Mahi noticed how their eyes met. Both immediately blushed. Her hands shook, holding the tray. His hands shook taking the tea. Then she turned to Mahi. 'Oh, a cup of tea, this will refresh us,' Mahi said with a reassuring smile. Then Esmat walked to the door, leaving quickly. She caught Ezat's eye before she closed the door, as she closed her eyes sparkled. At that instant Mahi knew that those two had fallen in love.

On the engagement day a small party was organised and Esmat was taken an engagement ring, an outfit, and some delicacies to eat. After that Ezat visited her frequently, once or twice a week, and had meals with her family, although they were never left alone. Gradually the wedding preparations got underway. The wedding day was a beautiful summer's day, and all the preparations were complete. Tables and chairs had been set out in the garden, a stage was made over the pool for the orchestra. The garden was full of flowers, and indoors there were bouquets everywhere. Their colours and scent filled the atmosphere, it was dazzling. Visitors began to arrive and gradually the house filled up with family, friends old and new, and, of course, Mash Ihia. People were sitting in the garden, on the balcony, in the roof garden. The orchestra was playing, the singer was singing and the people were clapping and dancing along with the music.

That night, Mahi, who had been in charge of organising the wedding, was feeling on top of the world. She was bubbly and happy as she moved around welcoming everyone, looking after the visitors and offering them sweets and cakes. She was behind the whole show from the start, advising, instructing, consulting, overseeing the whole thing. She was filled with energy, glowing with enthusiasm, her newly gained independence and her acceptance again by the family had given her new life, as she had proved once more to the world her capabilities, her strength. This had earned her enormous respect from the whole community. Both Khadijeh and Khoshghadam were visiting for the wedding. For Khoshghadam it was her first time in Teheran and she was overwhelmed by all the new things she was seeing there. She stood at Mahi's side at the wedding, being introduced to the many guests. She felt very proud of Mahi. Khadijeh accompanied her brother and her great-aunt, Ghadamkhir, to fetch the bride. 'I feel this is the highest point in my life,' she had said earlier on to Mahi. 'I feel so happy, so complete, I have never felt this way before, it is unique.'

'Highest point,' Mahi laughed, 'you don't know what is ahead. The highest point maybe yet to come, sister! Life is full of surprises, this is the beauty of it, you just don't know what is ahead.'

'No, I am sure. For me it is the highest point, now, this very moment. Now I can go completely satisfied.'

'Go where?' Mahi laughed at the top of her voice, putting her arms round her and hugging her tightly. 'You are staying with me for a while yet. I am not letting you go back to that village, not yet, there is a lot more to show you.'

'I feel so happy, sister,' Khadijeh muttered between tears and laughter. 'Seeing my daughter so happy with her handsome husband, having her own home which I never had, seeing you happy with everything that you have now achieved, seeing my brother so well-established, mother so fulfilled. I feel so lucky to have experienced all this. I feel that living these moments has made all my past suffering worthwhile.' At this, both sisters cried, hugging each other tight.

People kept watch for the bride's arrival, from the top of the roof, on the balcony, through the windows and out on the street. Then suddenly the first sighting came from the roof top. In the first car were bride and bridegroom. In the second car was Mamad-Ali, Ghadamkhir and Khadijeh, and in the third, some of the bride's family. Many other cars had joined them along the way, making it into a big procession, blowing their horns continuously and so drawing out more people to watch the procession. The streets were packed with spectators and well-wishers.

The orchestra played the special tune for their arrival. Esmat was received by the immediate family at the entrance, Mahi, Hasan and Habib. Sweets and coins were thrown over the couple's head and children rushed from every direction to collect them. Everyone cheered as they were led to a special sitting area in the centre of the garden so that all the guests could have a good view of them.

The house vibrated with laughter. Now, the celebration was in full swing. Roghiieh turned to Mahi and Khadijeh, her voice was trembling with excitement. 'Come on girls. Mahi – I wish I could speak Turkish and Farsi like you. New visitors have come and I don't know which language they are talking in.' Khadijeh couldn't speak Turkish or Farsi either but Mahi had mastered them both. She chatted freely in Kurdish one moment, Turkish the next, and then Farsi. They could hear Mash Ihia's laughter and chatter welcoming people, introducing himself and them to others.

'He sounds like the Master of Ceremonies,' Mahi said, and the three women roared with laughter.

Roghiieh felt so proud that her family home was giving

so much pleasure to so many people. 'This event will be the main talking point for a long time to come! I'm sure the news will travel back to the village and all the villages around, and be retold for generations to come – the story of Ezatollah's wedding day. This is so wonderful, having all my family and all my old friends here with me tonight, and it's all thanks to you Mahi – you've done so well!' With this, she took her daughter in her arms and embraced her.